Acknowledgements

Savii Digital Crypto and Blockchain Marketing agency focuses on the world's of cryptocurrency, blockchain and ITO/ICO promotion. Our international team of highly experienced crypto and blockchain marketing professionals are dedicated to teaching you about this space, and we love what we do for a living.

We would like to thank the entire team in the making of this book, but also give special thanks to Mihkel Šorin, our Content Director, and an amazingly talented individual who proves that Shakespeare is not the only gifted writer to have ever existed; Jovan Lazarević, our Creative Director, and one of the most talented graphic designers ever to grace the earth; and Raido Rentnik, our Media Director, who has the magic touch in making every finished product look like it just came off the assembly floor at Ferrari.

Thank you everyone. We could not have done this without you.

Sincerely,

Aviva Õunap
CEO
Savii Digital

Introduction

The popularity of the blockchain has seen rapid growth. More and more people are talking about this emerging technology than ever before as they believe that it has the potential to change the world for the better.

This book is meant as an introduction to the world of blockchain. It is not an in-depth technical field manual for programmers and developers who want to develop their own blockchain. It is meant to simplify the complex world of blockchain, so everyone can understand how it functions and gain knowledge about this topic.

You will also find that this book has a lot of examples that are simplified and in plain English, which are later tied together with the functions of blockchain and its terms. We will talk about how it works, what goes into it, what are the things that give it its unique characteristics, how it was created, and all the other questions you might have about blockchain technology but were afraid to ask.

People usually make mistakes because of their lack of knowledge. This book will help you educate yourself so that you can avoid the mistakes many people are making.

After finishing this book, you will be able to understand the concepts of blockchain technology, and happily engage in conversations with your new found knowledge.

CRYPTO
AND BLOCKCHAIN
FOR BEGINNERS

Ple
sho

ww

Rer

Tex
spe

Table of Contents

Blockchain 8

Introduction to Blockchain 8

Decentralization 8

Structure and Immutability 9

Transparency and Anonymity 9

Cryptography 9

Benefits 10

Disadvantages 10

Why Should I Care? 11

Case Study #1 - Transactions on the Blockchain 12

Case Study #2 - General Data Protection Regulation (GDPR) 14

Case Study #3 - The Equifax Breach 16

History 17

Electronic Cash 17

Smart Contracts 18

Bitcoin 18

Blockchain 2.0 18

Blockchain Today 19

Case Study #4 - Becoming e-Estonian 20

Case Study #5 - Banking the Unbanked 21

Cryptocurrencies 23

Introduction 23

Technology 23

Criminals 24

Accessing Cryptocurrencies and Wallets 24

Public and Private Keys 25

Tokens or Coins or Both? 25

Volatility of Cryptocurrencies and Who Controls the Price 26

Creation of a Personal Token/Coin 26

Bitcoin [BTC] 27

Ethereum [ETH] 28

Ripple [XRP] 29

Bitcoin Cash [BCH] 30

Cardano [ADA] 31

Litecoin [LTC] 32

NEO [NEO] 33

Stellar [XLM] 34

Monero [XMR] 35

EOS [EOS] 36

Dash [DASH] 37

IOTA [MIOTA] 38

NEM [XEM] 39

Case Study #6 - What is Gas? 40

Case Study #7 - SegWit 44

Smart Contracts **46**

What are Smart Contracts? 46

Concept 46

Benefits of Smart Contracts 47

Example 47

Uses for Smart Contracts 48

Conclusion 48

Cryptography **49**

Introduction 49

Uses 49

How it Works 50

Encryptions and Keys — 50

Hashing — 51

What's the Difference Between Hashing and Encryption? — 52

Multisig – Multi Signature Cryptography — 52

Hybrid Cryptography — 53

Conclusion — 53

ITOs and ICOs — **54**

What are ITOs/ICOs? — 54

Why are Some Countries Banning ITOs/ICOs? — 55

Conclusion — 55

How to Choose an ICO to Invest in — **56**

Funds Raised With ICOs in 2016 vs 2017 — 56

ICOs by Category in 2018 — 57

Scammers — 57

Phishing and Fake ICOs — 58

What to Look for Before Investing in ICOs — 58

Conclusion — 61

Transactions on the Blockchain — **62**

Introduction — 62

Transactions, Hash Function and Hash Value — 63

Understanding a Bitcoin Transaction — 64

Block Headers, Mining and Rewards — 65

Mekle Tree — 66

Blockchain Blocks — 67

Mining in Bitcoin — 68

Transactions — 68

Problems With Mining — 69

Blockchains and Algorithms — **70**

Rapid Fire Q&A — **74**

Conclusion — **77**

Blockchain

Introduction to Blockchain

The blockchain is a digital ledger that is run by a network of computers working in a Peer-to-Peer (P2P) configuration. This means it is a collection of data and transactions that are stored and processed by computers around the world, all working together. This configuration uses the network of computers and cryptography to create a system that is secure, transparent and at the same time anonymous (don't worry if this doesn't make sense right now. We will explain it all in detail in this book).

There are two terms that you will need to understand – centralized platforms and decentralized platforms. With centralized platforms, data is required to pass through one singular point. This means that you cannot physically send or receive any information without it going through that one single point, which is often a server or hub. A great example of a centralized platform is Google, or almost any major bank. There are some centralized blockchains, too.

Decentralized platforms do not require information to pass through one single point. Instead, information is stored on many computers in the network, creating a peer-to-peer (P2P) network configuration. Examples of a decentralized platform are Bitcoin or Ethereum.

Decentralization

Decentralization is the main factor with regards to the security of the blockchain. As previously explained, decentralization means that instead of one centralized server holding all of the information, there are many computers around the world that store a copy of this information.

This makes losing information almost impossible because it is quite unlikely that all of the independent computers around the globe will crash simultaneously and lose your data. Even if one computer in the network crashes, there will still be plenty of computers that hold a copy of the information, keeping your data safe and secure.

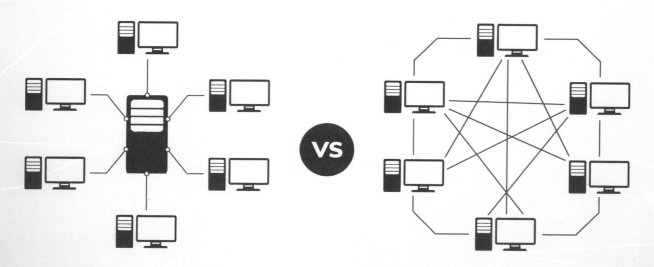

CENTRALIZED VS DECENTRALIZED

Structure and Immutability

The word 'blockchain' is a derivative of two words – 'block' and 'chain'. All of the data that is broadcast to the blockchain is put into blocks, which are subsequently linked to the previous block, creating a chronological order of blocks – or a 'blockchain'.

This chronological order of transactions is immutable, meaning that once something is broadcast and recorded on the blockchain, it cannot be altered. Once information is recorded on the blockchain, it is set in stone, and it can no longer be changed. This ensures that no-one can change the history to their liking. It is there to stay.

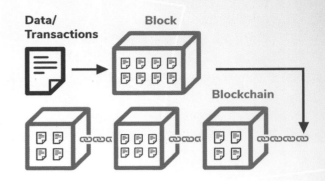

Transparency and Anonymity

All of the information about transactions on the blockchain is transparent and public, except for the users' personal information and the contents of their messages. This means that although all of the transactions are easily seen, the individuals who made the transactions are completely anonymous (the users are only identified by usernames or user IDs).

This transparency of information makes it possible for the network to verify the transactions made on the blockchain, whilst anonymity gives the user's peace of mind that no one can see their private information.

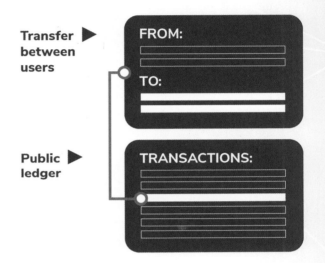

Cryptography

One of the tools used in blockchain technology to keep data safe is cryptography. This is a mathematical practice used to keep data hidden from third parties. This practice uses complex mathematical processes to encrypt information and keep it away from prying eyes, and these encryptions can only be decrypted by using certain keys. It is similar to when children create their own language to keep secrets from parents, but a more advanced version. We have a separate chapter for cryptography that goes more in depth.

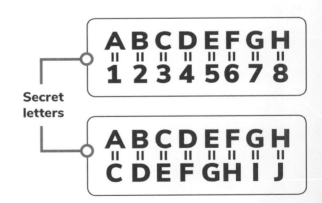

The combination of decentralization, cryptography, and transparency gives a blockchain its unique characteristics. The decentralization aspect provides security and keeps data safe, while transparency gives the validating role to the underlying network of computers, successfully eliminating third-parties who, up until now, did the validation themselves. Cryptography allows a situation where information about transactions can be broadcast to everyone, while personal information about the sender is never revealed.

Advantages of Blockchain

Security – blockchain's decentralization makes the information stored on the blockchain incredibly secure, because a copy of the information is kept on many computers across the world, and not on one centralized server or computer .

High transaction speeds – blockchain also increases transaction speeds, as there are no lengthy confirmation times and the transactions move directly to the recipient, and not through multiple middlemen.

Anonymity – the use of cryptography keeps users' personal information and messages sent through the blockchain secret.

Accessibility – blockchain does not need any physical institutions to function. The only requirement is a connection to the internet.

Disadvantages of Blockchain

Database size – blockchain is not meant to store and send terabytes worth of data, as the network of computers doesn't have enough storage to hold vast amounts of data. So it's mainly used for transactions, not as a cloud storage platform.

Unexplored – as blockchain technology is relatively new, its full potential, as well as some of its pain points, are yet to be explored and solved.

Misinformation – the amount of false information about blockchain technology has been decreasing, but there are still sources that give misleading information.

Rapid change and volatility – the blockchain world is changing almost every day. Most noticeable is the volatility of cryptocurrencies. They can fluctuate a lot, meaning that people can gain, or lose a lot of money.

Scams – the misinformation and the lack of knowledge surrounding blockchain, cryptocurrencies and ICOs mean that people can be taken advantage of too easily. People want to be a part of the rapid growth and profits that many have experienced in the cryptoworld and therefore can get pulled into possible scams.

Why Should I Care?

Are you saying to yourself, "Okay, I understand the main concept behind the blockchain, but why should I care?"

Well, there are a number of reasons why you should care. Let's expand on some of these reasons.

1 Imagine you have a friend who's visiting a foreign country. One day she calls you and tells you all about the wonderful times she is having, but she has miscalculated her expenditures and now has no money left. She asks you to send her some money and as a good friend, you agree to send her some money through a bank transfer.

You make the transaction and you notice that the transaction takes 2 days to reach your friend and above that, the bank takes a considerable fee from the transaction. Because of the long transfer time, your friend won't be able to buy the souvenir she wanted.

If you would have used blockchain to make this transaction, then it would have reached your friend in minutes or seconds, and you would not have paid high fees.

2 If you really don't care about high-speed transactions and low fees, then maybe you do care about keeping your private information away from hackers. With the use of blockchain, you can be the boss of your own information. You can control who has access to your credit information and medical records, keeping your personal data safe from prying eyes.

Traditional, centralized databases are susceptible to hacks and breaches. This has already happened, multiple times. In 2017 one of the largest credit reporting companies in the world, Equifax, experienced a major data breach, in which over 145 million US citizens had their identity stolen.

3 Also, with blockchain, companies have the ability to create smart contracts, which they can use to automate their business, track their production and keep their data safe.

4 Start-ups can use blockchain as a crowdfunding solution to fund their ventures, known as ICOs (Initial Coin Offerings) or ITOs (Initial Token Offerings).

5 Blockchain can also be used to eliminate fraud from the world of NGOs, decrease corruption in the voting process (making voting more popular and trustworthy), plus create the means to bank the unbanked 2 billion people in the world, decreasing poverty.

The new possibilities presented by blockchain technology can make the world a better and more efficient place. Businesses could be more effective, faster and autonomous. People can transact with others across the world in seconds and data can be kept safe. And it doesn't end with that since new possibilities are found almost every day.

Case Study #1

How the Blockchain Helps You
Send Money Everywhere

This is a bank. It holds the information about its customers and their money. This information is stored in a giant server.

This is Mack. He is one of the bank's customers. He has $1000 stored in his bank account, which the bank keeps safe.

One day Mack receives a phone call from his mother, who is on a trip in Africa. She tells him about all of the wonderful times that she has had. It is the final day of her trip and she admits that she has miscalculated spending and no longer has enough money to buy a magnificent statue of a camel as a souvenir.

Mack is a great son and promises to send her some money so she can buy the camel statue. He opens his laptop and sends some money from his bank account. Surprisingly, he finds out that the bank takes a considerable fee for the transaction and it will take 3 days for the transaction to reach the destination, and by that time, Mack's mother's trip is already over.

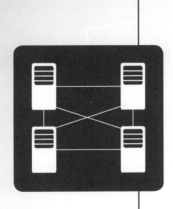

Could this have been done in another, more secure, faster and cheaper way?

This is where blockchain and cryptocurrencies come in.

Cryptocurrencies and their transactions are one of the most well-known use cases for the blockchain, which makes international banking a lot faster and cheaper.

If the bank has one giant centralized server that holds Mack's and all of the other clients' information and money, then blockchain technology uses many different computers all around the world, known as nodes, each of which stores a copy of the information. This is called decentralization. It makes the system much more secure and less susceptible to hacks and crashes. If one of the nodes in the network crashes, nothing happens, because the other nodes that all hold the same data are still running. If the bank's server crashes, then all of the transactions are delayed until the server is up and running again. Also, if someone wants to hack into Mack's account and steal all of his money, he would have to hack into every node at the exact same time, while stealing money from a bank would require him to hack into only one giant server.

If Mack creates a cryptocurrency transaction and sends some money to his mother, the nodes in the network will first check if Mack has enough money to conduct such a transaction, and if he does, then the transaction is bundled up with other transactions that happened at the same time. These bundles, known as blocks, are confirmed by nodes that in addition to holding the data, create reliable seals to the blocks. These nodes are called miners, and the seals that they provide make sure that once the blocks are confirmed, no-one can change the information in them afterwards. For this, the miners receive rewards in the form of cryptocurrencies. After the block is confirmed, it is attached to the chain of previous blocks, creating a chronological order of blocks, hence the name 'blockchain'. Once the blocks have been sealed and added to the blockchain, they can no longer be changed or corrupted.

Once the block with Mack's transaction is confirmed, the money pops up on his mother's account. Instead of waiting for days, Mack's mother now has enough time to buy the camel, before her trip finishes.

Mack is really happy that he could help his mother out and that he can use this new technology to keep his money safe and make international transactions that happen almost instantaneously, without paying enormous fees.

Case Study #2

Get Ready for General Data Protection Regulation (GDPR) With Blockchain

GDPR, short for General Data Protection Regulation, became a law on 25th of May, 2018. Since the amount of data breaches has been increasing in the recent years, new laws have had to be made in order to keep the citizens of the EU safe from identity thefts. The new regulation tightens up the existing laws on data protection and gathering of personal information.

This means that all organizations that deal with EU citizens' personal data have to review and make sure that this information is managed according to the European law and policies. This doesn't only apply to organizations located within EU, but to all of the organizations that have the data of EU citizens.

Personal information is any information that can be used to identify a person, including pictures, names, dates of birth, emails, phone numbers, bank details, medical records, etc.

If an organizations fails to change their record keeping systems to meet the recommendations of the law, then the possible fine for breaching GDPR is up to 4% of the organization's annual global turnover or €20 million. This penalty applies to both data controllers and data processors. The data controller is the party that creates the rules, the purpose and conditions of data collecting and processing (for example, a company), and the data processor is the party that stores and processes the data (data storage company).

In Short, the Main Changes in the Laws are:

Larger territorial jurisdiction – this law applies to every company that deals with information about EU citizens, no matter where the location of the company may be.

Penalty for non-compliance – organizations can be fined up to 4% of the organisation's annual global turnover or €20 million for breaching the regulation

Consent – the terms and conditions are strengthened and no longer can be full of legalese. The request for consent has to be clear, in plain language, easily accessible and distinguishable from other matters, with the purpose of data processing attached. The consent must be as easy to withdraw as it is to give.

Clarity – organisations have to state clearly why they require certain information. The information must be collected for specified purposes, kept secure, correct and, up-to-date, and it shouldn't be kept for longer than necessary.

Breach notifications – organisations are obliged to notify a breach in the system to a local Information Commissioner and their clients within 72 hours of first discovering the breach.

Right to access – people whose data is processed have the right to know where, how and for what their information is used. The organisation has to provide this information for the customer for free and he/she can transmit this information to another organisation.

Right to be forgotten – people whose data is processed have the right of having their information erased from the system unless there are legal reasons or it's in the public interest to store the data.

Privacy by Design and Data Protection Officers – organizations have to prioritize the security of their data bases from the ground up and must assign Data Protection Officers who make sure that data is held safely and will notify officials immediately in case of a breach.

The reason this regulation was made was because there have been more and more cases of breaches in large databases that hold people's personal information, leaving them susceptible to identity theft.

Many of these breaches could have been prevented with the use of decentralized and distributed databases – in other words, the blockchain. Blockchain technology was created for keeping personal data safe and secure. Blockchain technology uses networks of computers that all work together to store and validate information, creating a decentralized database. If one of the computers on the network crashes, then nothing happens to the information, because there are still many computers that hold the same data.

The information stored on the blockchain is cryptographically encrypted. The encrypted messages can only be decrypted with specific keys, and without the correct key it is practically impossible to decrypt the data. Decryption via brute force attacks, or by guessing every possible answer, would take millions of years.

The data stored on the blockchain is also transparent and public with the use of hashing. This mathematical function makes it possible to validate whether a document is correct and unaltered without having to see the content. These hashes can be verified by everybody participating in the network. This ensures that the data isn't corrupted, while keeping the message and the owner anonymous.

These properties can be implemented into any business, government organisation or NGO, making their services more secure and reliable. Blockchain as a Service (BAAS) is meant to provide organisations with improved security, transparency, trust and traceability in the face of decentralization, making their organisation and data less susceptible to hacks and data breaches.

Blockchain Benefits:

Businesses can move their record keeping onto the blockchain in order to keep the personal information of their customers and employees safe and secure.

Health records can be stored on the blockchain without the fear of losing them or having them stolen.

Access to personal information can be accurately shared, without unwanted third parties being able to access that data.

Ownership of a property or a document can be proved in seconds, without revealing the content inside.

With General Data Protection Regulation, organizations having to make sure that their data processing protocols are up-to-date with the new laws. Personal data has to be kept secure and the best approach in doing so would be to utilize blockchain technology. The combination of cryptography and decentralization is the ultimate way to keep data protected, and keep in line with the rules and upcoming legislation.

Case Study #3

The Equifax Breach in the USA

Equifax, one of the nation's three main credit reporting agencies (the other two are Experian and TransUnion), announced on September 7, 2017 that they had a 'cybersecurity incident' that potentially impacted approximately 143 million U.S. consumers. In other words, they were hacked.

The cybersecurity firm, Mandiant, completed the forensic portion of its investigation on the incident by the beginning of October 2017, and announced that approximately 2.5 million additional U.S. consumers were impacted, raising the total number of victims to 145.5 million, which is over 40% of the U.S. population.

Based on the company's investigation, the 'unauthorized access' – or hacking - occurred from mid-May through July 2017. The information accessed included names, Social Security numbers, birth dates, addresses and, driver's license numbers. In addition, credit card numbers for approximately 209,000 U.S. consumers, and certain dispute documents with personal identifying information for approximately 182,000 U.S. consumers, were accessed. As part of its investigation of this application vulnerability, Equifax also identified unauthorized access to limited personal information for certain UK and Canadian residents.

Criminals exploited the U.S. based website application to gain access to certain files. Criminals now have all of the information they need to harm individuals and they can decide to use it whenever they want.

The Equifax hack serves as a prime example of how centralized databases and servers create massive vulnerabilities for consumers. One single company's system exposed sensitive information, potentially compromising the identity, and safety, of nearly half the country.

Several specialists have now been suggesting that using blockchain technology would have kept consumers' data completely safe.

Jason Bloomberg, who has dubbed himself 'a sceptic– primarily around Bitcoin, but for blockchain as well', claimed in Forbes that an open sourced distributed ledger would solve the problem fast. In addition, he stated, that a decentralized platform would give the extra safety and security that Equifax was lacking.

Building the solutions to these problems using blockchain technology allows more than safety and security. There are so many more plusses, including transaction speeds and transparency that make a decentralized solution the only solution going forward for every company.

"The whole SSN as identifier regime needs to be scrapped," says Eduard Goodman, global privacy officer at the identity theft protection firm CyberScout. "As we see more and more issues with the centralization of data, we see the need to implement different schemes for different uses—biometrics for in-person interactions and transactions, and some form of advanced encryption or blockchain technologies for online activities. The solutions are already in front of our eyes."

According to Jerry Cuomo, Vice President of Blockchain Technologies at IBM, consumers have sovereign authority over their personal information when operating on blockchain platforms, since transactions are securely verified by permissioned participants. Bypassing centralized servers and databases will spread consumer information across secured peer-to- peer networks protected by layers of cryptography. Incidents like the Equifax hack lend credence to the benefits of blockchain in enhancing cybersecurity.

1   https://www.equifaxsecurity2017.com

2   https://www.forbes.com/sites/jasonbloomberg/2017/10/06/can-blockchain-solve-the-equifax-identity-morass-heres-how/#586acd296a73

3   https://www.wired.com/story/the-equifax-breach-exposes-americas-identity-crisis/

4   https://www.freightwaves.com/news/2017/9/12/lessons-learned-from-equifax

History

The rapidly growing industry of the blockchain has been a popular topic of discussion in recent years. The incredible increase in Bitcoin's price has made many people interested in this emerging technology, and new applications using the blockchain are made almost every day. But where did it all start? A lot of sources connect the birth of blockchain with the invention of Bitcoin, but in reality, while Bitcoin incorporated all of the concepts and created a functioning system, the concepts and technologies behind it were described long before Bitcoin was born.

Electronic Cash

In 1983 a computer scientist and a cryptographer by the name of David Chaum came up with the idea behind eCash. He described eCash as anonymous cryptographic electronic money or electronic cash system, which could be used to transfer funds anonymously.

For that, he invented the blinding formula – a digital signing formula in which a message is hidden before being signed, making it possible to transfer a document that is signed by a third-party, without giving the third-party the ability to read the document. This invention introduced anonymity to payment systems and is the idea behind the use of public and private keys that are still used today.

The first time something resembling a blockchain was described was in the early 1990s.

In 1991 two scientists Stuart Haber and W. Scott Stornetta described time-stamping of digital documents and creating a network of users to store and validate cryptographically secured documents. This theory was described as a solution to eliminate the theft of documents and plagiarism.

To test their system, they created a network of computers which would validate and store the documents. They time-stamped the digital documents with the use of cryptography, which allowed the network of users to see if a document has been altered and to confirm the rightful owner of the documents. If someone tried to alter a document, it would be easily seen and the corrupt version of the document would be discarded.

This theory was further improved upon in 1992 by Dave Bayer, Stuart Haber, and W. Scott Stornetta by introducing Merkle trees into the mix. This introduced a new structure to how the documents were stored and made the protocol more effective, reducing the storage and the total computing power needed to validate transactions.

Smart Contracts

A few years later, in 1995 one of David Chaum's former employees, cryptographer Nick Szabo, came up with the idea of smart contracts. Smart contracts are essentially contracts that work on the blockchain. Nick Szabo himself compared smart contracts to vending machines – when enough money is put inside and a product is chosen, it triggers the machine to drop the specific product. Smart contracts are used to automate different contractual processes, making them partially or fully self-executing.

After he described the theory behind smart contracts, Nick designed a digital currency called Bit Gold that ran on a decentralized network, which is often called the precursor of Bitcoin. The main idea behind the system was that when transactions are made they are broadcast to the network where computers solve mathematical challenges to validate a transaction. Once a computer solves a puzzle, the answer is broadcast to the network where computers verify the answer. If the answer is approved by the network, the transaction is made and the puzzle is put away. All of the following puzzles are tied together, creating a string of challenges. This system had many unsolved issues and loose ends and was thus never implemented.

Bitcoin

After many years, the first distributed blockchain was conceptualized by an anonymous group or a person using the name Satoshi Nakamoto (no-one still knows his/her/their identity). Satoshi Nakamoto published a white-paper called 'Bitcoin: A Peer-to-Peer Electronic Cash System' in 2008, describing the idea behind Bitcoin – electronic currency that is run on blockchain technology and that is not controlled by any central authority. The following year, in 2009, the concept was made a reality with the creation of Bitcoin. This marked the beginning of public blockchains and cryptocurrencies.

> **Fun fact:** There are people who vigorously investigate the origin of Satoshi Nakamoto and who this person or group could be. It has gone as far as major media outlets claiming they have found out who the inventor is, such as when Newsweek claimed that a man by the name of Dorian Nakamoto is Satoshi, which greatly disrupted the man's personal life, and triggered him to launch a lawsuit against Newsweek.
>
> There are also claims that the inventor of Bit Gold, Nick Szabo, is Satoshi Nakamoto, because the two share a similar writing style and use the same operating systems.

Blockchain 2.0

With the invention of Bitcoin, the popularity of cryptocurrencies and blockchain took off. More and more cryptocurrencies were made and new applications for blockchain technology were developed.

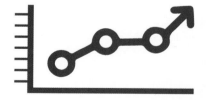

The main concept behind Bitcoin was that it acted as a currency for the internet, allowing users to make transactions without the need of middlemen, like banks, but that was it. More and more new uses for the blockchain were developed, and by the year 2014, this technology advanced to the point where people could use the blockchain beyond digital currencies. This was called Blockchain 2.0. These advancements meant that in addition to making transactions with digital currencies, users could create smart contracts, companies could create certificates for sending their owners dividends, and people could easily authenticate and sign documents. And this was only the beginning!

Blockchain Today

Blockchain technology has evolved tremendously. People working on blockchain technology developed new applications for almost every day, solving problems many experts thought could never be solved.

Blockchain is showing its usefulness in almost every sector of business, starting from the use of cryptography to seal digital documents and prove ownership, to being able to track the can of tuna throughout its journey, from sea to supermarket - from first being caught, to processing, logistics, shipping, and ending up on your plate.

Blockchain Food Traceability

From an idea on paper, to a currency that has risen from nothing to over thousands of dollars the span of 8 years, we are now able to trade different cryptocurrencies in real-time, and use cryptocurrencies to buy products in physical and online stores. What the future holds for blockchain technology is impossible to predict. It might be the thing that changes the world forever, or not. Only time will tell.

Blockchain as a Service Covers:

SMART CONTRACTS

 Supply Chain

 Digital Rights

 Wagers

 Escrow

 ERP

DIGITAL CURRENCY

 E-Commerce

 Global Payments

 Remittance

 P2P Lending

 Microfinance

SECURITIES

 Equity

 Private Markets

 Debt

 Crowdfunding

 Derivates

RECORD KEEPING

 Healthcare

 Title Records

 Ownership

 Voting

 Intellectual Property

Case Study #4

Estonia's National Blockchain and e-Solutions - Becoming e-Estonia

Estonia was the first country in the world to implement blockchain technology on a national basis. It started building up its information society in the year 1997. At this time, there was no digital information being collected about Estonians, and the general population had neither access to the Internet, nor devices with which to use it.

After years of development, Estonia rose to the forefront of technological advancement as a nation. In 2005, Estonia introduced internet voting in a nationwide election, becoming the first country to do so. By this time, Estonia had also already developed its digital identity, e-tax and e-governance solutions.

Cyberattacks and Blockchain

On April 27, 2007, Estonia became the first country to be cyber attacked on a national level. The attacks targeted the websites of Estonian organizations, including the Estonian parliament, banks, ministries, newspapers and broadcasters. Most of these attacks consisted of DDoS attacks, ping floods and spam bots, and targeted entire organizations as well as individuals.

Estonia understood that the risk of cyberattacks will always be a part of being an information society, but the nationwide attacks acted as a serious wake-up call to remind Estonia, as well as every other country, how important cybersecurity is.

In response to this cyberattack, NATO created a Cooperative Cyber Defence Centre of Excellence in Tallinn, the capital city of Estonia, and Estonia started testing blockchain technology to protect the country against future attacks.

Blockchain testing began in 2008, even before the release of the famous white paper by Satoshi Nakamoto that described the concept of Bitcoin and attached the name "blockchain" to the technology.

Since 2012, blockchain has been in use by Estonia to protect their national data, e-services and smart devices both in the public and private sectors.

E-solutions

Examples of Estonia's e-solutions include the famous e-residency program that allows foreigners to have a digital identity in Estonia, allowing them to access its solutions, and even open a business in Estonia without any problems.

Another example is the e-Health record system which was launched in 2008. Over 95% of data generated by hospitals, doctors and other institutions in the healthcare industry are digitalized and protected by blockchain technology. Every Estonian citizen has their own e-health record, which can be shared with hospitals and personal doctors. This makes Estonians residents the owners of their health records, while increasing security and cutting costs.

Estonia is the perfect example to illustrate the benefits of blockchain technology not only from an individual's perspective, but also from the standpoint of a country. The use of blockchain increases the security of the nation's databases as well as saves billions of euros in costs.

Banking the Unbanked

The world of technology has seen rapid growth in recent years. According to statistics from Internet World Stats, over half of the world's population has access to the internet, and it has grown from 0.4% in 1995 to 51.7% in 2017.

Although the world is clearly evolving at an exponential pace, there are still major problems in the rural parts of the world. Even though there have been over 700 million new bank accounts opened from 2011-2014, there are still over 2 billion people unbanked, meaning they don't have access to any kind of financial institution. Having no bank account makes having financial stability much more difficult. Imagine a storeowner in Yemen, who has worked hard for years and earns his money daily. In Yemen 93.5% of the people do not have a bank account and neither does our hardworking shopkeeper. What does that mean for him?

It means that every day, when his working hours are over, he has to risk his whole day's earnings when he has to transport the cash from his store to his home. Even if he did not get mugged when passing through shady neighbourhoods on his way home, he still has to keep his savings under his mattress, as he is susceptible to robbery. In addition, he has almost no opportunity to get a loan to expand his business and contribute to the country's economy. The only way he can get a loan is to get it from other people, who will have him paying unimaginable interest for his loan.

In another example, we have a mother with an 8-year-old daughter who lives in Guinea, where the unbanked population makes up over 90% of the country's population. In order to provide the best possible education for her daughter and allow her the ability to make a respectable living in the future, the mother has put her daughter to study at the local school. But because she does not have a bank account, she has to pay the school fees in cash, waiting in line with the other parents to make the payment, losing many hours from work.

Now in order to further facilitate this trend of financial inclusion, the world of finance has to become even more affordable, transparent and accessible. This is where blockchain technology comes in. Every day in the cryptocurrency sector we have the brightest minds on the planet working on problems many experts thought could never be solved, while using some of the most innovative technology the world has ever seen. Blockchain technology holds the keys to reaching the 2 billion unbanked, bringing transparency and justice to a broken financial system, stamping out corruption and exploitation.

Everyone should realize that a collaborative blockchain is not only a network of computers around the world, but also an ecosystem of humans who are behind the computers. The mixture of humans and computers around the world, working together gives means for supercharging the innovation and advancements in the industry, creating value for the world to use.

This is the problem we face right now in the business world. We're still stuck in the same zero-sum mentality we inherited from the traditional economy: "We don't collaborate, we compete!", and many think it is time that changed. Only through realizing the true potential of collaboration on the blockchain, can we start eliminating the problems with finance and poverty around the world.

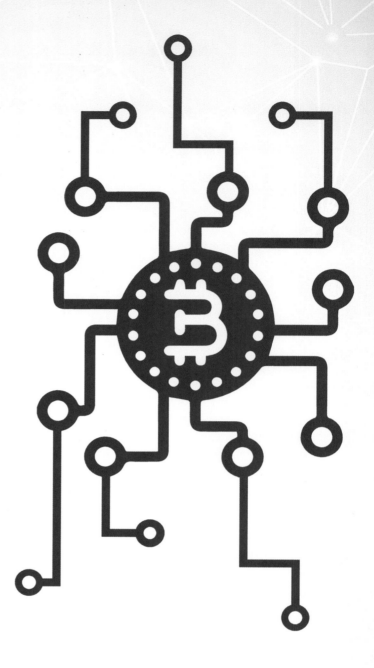

In conclusion, the world of blockchain gives us endless opportunities to change the world for the better by providing financial solutions for even the most rural parts of the world, giving them increased financial stability and security. But in order to do so, we have to opt for a more collaborative way of doing business.

Cryptocurrencies

Introduction

You most probably have heard about Bitcoin and stories about people who got rich almost overnight with their cryptocurrency investments, or maybe you have heard how people have lost a lot of their money on crypto exchange, or have been scammed. But what exactly are cryptocurrencies and why are some people getting a ridiculous return on investment while others lose almost all of their investment?

Cryptocurrencies are the best-known feature of blockchain technology. They are known as the 'cash of the internet' because they allow users to make transactions without the need for middlemen and without leaving a trace.

The main reason why cryptocurrencies have become so popular is mostly because of Bitcoin and its exponential increase in price. The initial growth in the price attracted more people to the platform, which in return increased the price, even more, thus creating a seemingly endless loop of price growth and the increase in the user base.

Fun fact: In the beginning, accumulating cryptocurrencies was easy and cheap since the prices were low and there was no competition. There was one case where a man bought 1500 Bitcoin for only $25. After not seeing any benefit from holding them, he threw away the hard-drive containing them, only to realize some years later that he basically threw away millions of dollars. At the time of writing 1500BTC is a little over $10 million.

Technology

Cryptocurrencies are run on blockchain technology. This means that all of the transactions are validated and recorded by the underlying network of computers. This enables transactions to take place in milliseconds and because it doesn't require big and expensive databases to be built, it reduces transaction fees. In addition, the decentralization provides security and immutability, giving everyone accurate information about past transactions.

Criminals

Before continuing, let's get one of the main questions out of the way.

"But aren't cryptocurrencies meant for drug dealers and money launderers?"

This is usually the main reason people think twice before talking about the benefits of cryptocurrencies and anonymity. The main concern is that, because cryptocurrency transactions are anonymous and can't be traced back to the person of origin, it makes it perfect for criminals to send and receive money for their criminal activities, without having the fear of getting caught. This statement isn't false. There have been cases of criminals using cryptocurrencies to make transactions.

But this problem is nothing new. After all, criminals have been around for a long time and they have used every other possible way of transferring money. Who hasn't seen a movie where a criminal opens a suitcase full of cold, hard cash? Saying that cryptocurrencies are only for criminals is almost the same as saying that cars are for criminals because they are used during many criminal activities.

Aside from that, most of the platforms that deal with cryptocurrency payments require high levels of verification and identification, meaning that before being able to start buying, selling, and transferring crypto, users have to prove their identity and provide certain documents to validate themselves. This protocol greatly decreases the likelihood of criminals using these platforms.

Accessing Cryptocurrencies and Wallets

In order to start sending and receiving cryptocurrencies, you first have to create an account on a cryptocurrency exchange and get it verified. The verification process, called KYC or Know Your Customer, requires certain documents to identify the user including bill statements and government issued ID. This process ensures that people who should not deal with crypto cannot use the platform and do something foolish. After getting verified, you can make your first purchase.

To hold your cryptocurrencies you have to own a cryptocurrency wallet. This wallet is digital and does not physically hold these coins and tokens, but instead, it proves your ownership of your coins and tokens, exactly like your regular internet bank account. It also contains your public and private keys, which are used for sending and receiving money.

There are mainly two types of wallets, "hot" and "cold" wallets. Hot wallets are those which are connected to the internet. This allows fast and easy access, but on the downside, hot wallets are not the safest. Cold wallets are not connected to the internet, meaning they are more secure because of that, but can't be accessed everywhere. There are also hybrid wallets, which can be connected to the internet, but don't rely on them.

For example, online wallets are purely hot wallets, and they are dependent on internet access. An example of a cold wallet would be a paper wallet, which can be on a piece of paper that has your public and private keys on it in the form of QR codes, or a USB stick that has your wallet on it. Desktop and mobile wallets are examples of hybrid wallets, as they work with and without an internet connection.

Public and Private Keys

Once you have your first cryptocurrencies in your wallet, then you probably want to know how to send your coins or tokens and how does this process work.

In order to make transactions, the money and the information has to be encrypted so no-one other than the recipient has access to receive this money or use the information sent. This is where the public and private keys come into play.

Public and private keys are long numbers with a lot of digits that are tied to your account. They are completely unique for every account.

Public keys, like the name implies, are visible for everybody, while private keys should be kept secret. The function of the keys is that if data is encrypted with someone's public key, then it can only be decrypted with this person's private key and vice-versa.

For example, if Jim wants to send Susan sensitive data, then Jim uses Susan's public key to encrypt the data and then sends it to Susan. Once Susan receives the encrypted document, she can use her private key to decrypt the message. If for some reason the message also ends up in the hands of David by mistake, he wouldn't have any means of decrypting the message, because he doesn't know Susan's private key. Thus the information is kept safe.

Tokens or Coins or Both?

Now you might be wondering, what are coins, what are tokens and what's the difference?

Coins are the native cryptocurrencies of blockchain protocols – Ether is the coin for Ethereum protocol, Bitcoin is the coin of the Bitcoin protocol. These coins are meant to be used as a payment method for products and services.

Tokens are cryptocurrencies that are built on top of an already existing protocol – the OMG token is a token built on the Ethereum protocol. These tokens can be used for more than payments. For example, tokens can be used for holding voting power or act like shares from a company.

Coins are determined by the protocol and exist on the base level, while tokens are determined by the smart contracts that are built on top of these protocols. You can think of coins as the mother and tokens as her daughters. Although they are different, in everyday situations, tokens and coins are often used as synonyms.

Another term you will hear is the word Altcoin. Altcoin is a combination of two words: 'alt' and 'coin'; alt is the abbreviation for the word alternative, and 'coin' denotes currency. Together they cover the category of cryptocurrencies that are alternatives to Bitcoin. These concern all coins and tokens that came after the initial release of the famous Bitcoin, the first decentralized cryptocurrency.

Volatility of Cryptocurrencies, and Who Controls the Price

The value of cryptocurrencies are based on the supply and demand of the marketplace. If there are a lot of people selling, but not a lot of people buying, then the price drops. When there are a lot of people wanting to buy, but there are no sellers, then the price increases.

The same thing applies to traditional FIAT currencies (government issued monies like USD, EUR or CNY, but what makes the cryptocurrency market so volatile? If cryptocurrencies are based on the same principles as the traditional currencies are, then why don't we see news about the USD increasing 20% in value in a week? The answer is in the market cap – how much money is in these systems.

Since cryptocurrencies are still relatively new, then there isn't a lot of money in this system yet. This means that the prices are more affected by buying and selling, making them more likely to fluctuate.

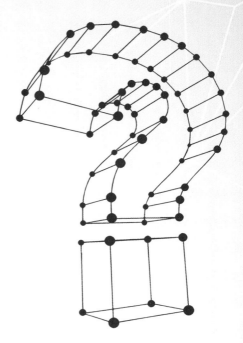

The current market cap for all of the cryptocurrencies in the world combined was around 200 billion USD (in 2017). For comparison, the market cap was around $420 trillion USD at the time of writing. Because the volatility of currencies is closely tied to the amount of money in the market, it means that if the amount of money in cryptocurrencies increases, the volatility of them decreases.

This volatility makes it easy to accumulate more money when thought through, in other words, buying low and selling high, but it also makes it easy to lose a lot of money by buying high and selling low. The high volatility means that the price difference between the highs and lows can be quite large.

Creation of a Personal Token/Coin

"Wow, cryptocurrencies seem like fun! How can I create my own?"

Well, it depends on how complex of a system you want to create. There are different ways you can approach this. The most difficult path would be to develop your own blockchain protocol with its own coin. This requires extensive programming and development skills. Another way would be to alter an already existing open-source protocol to your liking. Or you could build your token on top of an existing blockchain protocol. This still requires a lot of knowledge about blockchain technology, although not as much as building it from scratch. And the easiest way would be to create your own vanity coin on a platform that provides such a service. This coin won't have any functionality, besides being entertaining and fun to send to your friends as a joke.

> **Fun fact:** In 2013 Dogecoin was launched as a joke. It was meant for fun and entertainment, but quickly gained popularity and at the time of writing Dogecoin has a market cap of around $130M.

Once you have created your coin or token, another difficult task stands in your way. You have to get enough people on board to make your cryptocurrency worth something - or you could just leave it at that and send those coins to your friends for fun.

Bitcoin [BTC]

Bitcoin is the world's first cryptocurrency, described in 2008 by an unknown person or a group called Satoshi Nakamoto.

The purpose of Bitcoin is to become an alternative to traditional payment solutions, offering world-wide payments incredibly fast and cheap, without having a central authority, like the bank, controlling the transactions. Instead it is controlled by computers around the world who validate all of the transactions in a P2P (Peer to Peer) fashion.

Bitcoins are created in the process of "mining", which means that the computers, or miners, in the network solve complex mathematical puzzles to validate transactions, and whichever computer solves the puzzle the fastest is awarded an amount of Bitcoin, as well as transaction fees, as a reward. Of course, these fees and rewards go to the owners of the computers. This is also called the Proof-of-Work consensus algorithm, which is the most popular algorithm in the cryptocurrency world.

Interesting facts:

A lot of people have heard about Bitcoin, but have never heard about all of the other cryptocurrencies. Many people treat Bitcoin and cryptocurrency as synonyms.

While the information about the users is kept secret, the history of Bitcoin transactions is completely transparent, and everyone can see the amounts sent.

There are a finite number of Bitcoins – 21,000,000BTC. They are being mined and it is calculated that the last Bitcoin will be mined on 2140.

Bitcoin mining uses enough energy annually to power almost 4,000,000 average US households.

The first real world Bitcoin transaction happened on May 2010, when Laszlo Hanyecz bought 2 pizzas for 10,000BTC.

The current fee for a transaction that gets confirmed in about 1 hour is around $10 USD.

Bitcoin's team has developed a concept called Lightning Network that will hopefully solve the scalability problems, as well as high fees and slow speeds.

Whitepaper: https://bitcoin.org/bitcoin.pdf

Website: https://bitcoin.org/en/

Coinmarketcap: https://coinmarketcap.com/currencies/bitcoin/

Ethereum [ETH]

Ether is one of the top cryptocurrencies, proposed by Vitalik Buterin in 2013, as a next step in cryptocurrencies and blockchain. Ethereum is a blockchain-based, open-source smart contract platform. While the early cryptocurrencies, like Bitcoin, had only one functionality, P2P payments, Ethereum allows users to create smart contracts, issue their own tokens and run decentralized apps (DApps), making it possible to do a lot more things on the blockchain than before. Ethereum's open-source nature means that anyone can take the source code and build on top of it.

Smart contracts are basically programs that run on the blockchain and they make it possible for people to issue their own cryptocurrencies, launch ICOs (initial coin offerings), create apps that run on the blockchain and even automate companies, capable of functioning without human intervention.

Interesting facts:

"Ethereum" is the platform and the cryptocurrency is called "Ether" [ETH], but most of the time people use "Ethereum" for both the platform and the currency. Ether can be used for trading, for paying transaction fees and paying for Ethereum's services.

Ethereum is the most popular platform for launching ICOs, and around 50% of the ICOs are run on Ethereum's blockchain. These tokens are created on the ERC-20 protocol and are called ERC-20 tokens.

Ethereum currently uses the Proof-of-Work consensus algorithm, meaning computers use extensive computing power to validate transactions – also known as mining, but it is planning on moving to a Proof-of-Stake algorithm called Casper (where transactions are validated not by using computing power, but by having a stake – or an amount of tokens - in the system).

In 2016, there was a major mishap involving one of the ICOs on Ethereum platform. A company called The DAO raised $150M with its ICO. Since the code was public, it was hacked into, and someone claimed around $50M. This incident resulted in a split in the community and a hard-fork. Ethereum split into Ethereum and Ethererum Classic (the original Ethereum reversed the incident, while the Classic left the incident, because the idea of reversing the blockchain was against many enthusiasts' beliefs).

At the end of 2017, a decentralized app called CryptoKitties which is run on Ethereum's blockchain brought out the scalability issues with Ethereum, making it clear that before wide-spread adoption of this blockchain could take hold, work needs to be done on perfecting the system. So if your ETH transaction was late at the end of 2017, then you can blame the people who bought cats on the blockchain.

Whitepaper: https://github.com/ethereum/wiki/wiki/White-Paper

Website: https://www.ethereum.org/

Coinmarketcap: https://coinmarketcap.com/currencies/ethereum/

Ripple [XRP]

Ripple is the world's first enterprise blockchain solution for global payments. It connects banks, payment providers, digital asset exchanges and more through its network to provide frictionless global payments.

Instead of payments going through multiple banks when making an international payment (which could take days to finally be confirmed and are quite expensive), the transaction will go through the Ripple network. This means that all transactions take place directly between the sender's and recipient's banks, making the process a lot cheaper and faster.

One thing to note is that the word Ripple in the cryptoworld can mean three separate things. There's the Ripple platform for payments, then there's Ripple, the company that manages the Ripple platform, and finally there is Ripple [XRP], the native currency of the Ripple network. That's a lot to digest!

Ripple doesn't use Proof-of-Work to validate transactions. Running a Ripple node for validating transactions is not open to everybody like it is with most cryptocurrencies. Ripple chooses the nodes they trust to process these transactions. This means it's not truly decentralized like all of the other cryptocurrencies, but on the other hand, it makes the transactions a lot faster.

Interesting facts:

Ripple's concept was actually proposed in 2004, well before Bitcoin, but was not realized until 2012.

While Bitcoin processes around 4-7 transactions per second, Ripple has a transaction speed of around 1,500 transactions per second.

When making a transaction, a small amount of XRP that is used as the transaction fee (to protect against spam) is burned in the process. This means that no-one earns these fees and the supply of XRP decreases, making it increase in value.

Ripple is criticized by many blockchain evangelists because of its centralized characteristics.

Ripple's network is still in development, but they have already made a lot of partnerships with prominent financial companies.

Guide: https://ripple.com/files/ripple_solutions_guide.pdf

Website: https://ripple.com/

Coinmarketcap: https://coinmarketcap.com/currencies/ripple/

Bitcoin Cash [BCH]

Bitcoin Cash is a Bitcoin hard-fork that happened on the 1st of August, 2017. The fork was initiated because of scalability issues with the classic Bitcoin. Bitcoin Cash changed the size of the blocks from 1MB to 8MB, making it possible to process roughly around 60 transactions per second, compared to the 7 transactions per second by the classic Bitcoin, including the SegWit update. It also has lower transaction fees, compared to Bitcoin.

Bitcoin Cash didn't integrate the Segregated Witness (SegWit) protocol (see page 43). Furthermore, it has a stronger protection against replay attacks (which are a form of network attacks in which a valid data transmission is maliciously repeated or delayed), and the difficulty of the block mining has been adjusted to be faster than Bitcoin.

One main problem with Bitcoin Cash is that the increased block size makes it difficult for smaller miners (computers) to contribute, because they are not able to process this amount of data. The size of Bitcoin Cash's block sizes are 8MB each as compared to Bitcoin's 1MB, and both have 10 minute block times, so every 10 minutes there is eight times more information being saved on Bitcoin Cash's blockchain, making it faster than the traditional Bitcoin blockchain. This means over 1GB of new data every day.

Interesting facts:

Bitcoin Cash is the first successful Bitcoin hard-fork.

Everyone who had Bitcoin in their wallet during the hard-fork got the same amount of Bitcoin Cash for free.

Bitcoin Cash was created to become the P2P electronic cash system that Satoshi Nakamoto described in the Bitcoin whitepaper title page, which the traditional Bitcoin failed to become.

Bitcoin Cash's transactions are currently 100x's cheaper than Bitcoin transactions.

Website: https://www.bitcoincash.org/

Coinmarketcap: https://coinmarketcap.com/currencies/bitcoin-cash/

Cardano [ADA]

Cardano is considered a 3rd generation cryptocurrency, led by one of the founders of Ethereum, Charles Hoskinson. Cardano is a smart contract platform like Ethereum, but takes the idea to a new level by trying to solve issues with scalability, interoperability and sustainability of current cryptocurrencies. It is labelled as the first blockchain project that is based on scientific philosophy and built on academic research that has gone through detailed academic review and analysis.

Cardano is building its platform with both end-users and regulators in mind, by trying to find the middle ground between regulations, privacy and decentralization. The platform uniquely uses Haskel programming language that offers high degree of fault tolerance, which ensures that the code stays relevant and usable in the future.

Cardano is built on two layers – one is for registering the movement of ADA and the other one is for running smart contracts, which means more flexibility and security. Cardano is using their own Proof-of-Stake algorithm called Ouroboros, which will make transactions a lot faster as well as eliminating the need of storing the whole blockchain on every node. Ouroboros instead generates leader nodes who push the transactions.

Interesting facts:

Charles Hoskinson, the creator of Cardano and one of the founders of Ethereum, was one of the people who supported Ethereum Classic after the DAO incident. He was adamant that reversing the DAO hack was against the principles of blockchain technology.

Cardano is working on enabling cross chain transfers, making it possible to exchange, for example, ADA to Bitcoin directly through sidechains, eliminating the need to go through exchanges.

Cardano is working on their wallet (named Daedalus) that will be able to support multiple cryptocurrencies in the future.

Cardano is developing a system that allows different signature schemes to be added in the future. They are also looking to integrate quantum proof signatures (cryptographically secure digital signatures).

Cardano didn't write a white paper like all of the other cryptocurrencies. Instead, they presented a collection of design principles, engineering best practices and avenues for exploration.

Philosophy: https://www.cardanohub.org/en/philosophy/

Website: https://www.cardanohub.org/en/home/

Coinmarketcap: https://coinmarketcap.com/currencies/cardano/

Litecoin [LTC]

Litecoin is a cryptocurrency that like Bitcoin, offers peer-to-peer, near-instant, and almost zero cost payments to anyone in the world. Created by Charlie Lee who has worked for Google and Coinbase, Litecoin is an open source global payment network that is fully decentralized without any central authority. The network is secured by cryptography and emPoWers individuals to control their own finances.

Litecoin was inspired by Bitcoin and in technical details is nearly identical to the 'King of Cryptocurrencies'. The main differences between Litecoin and Bitcoin are in the confirmation time and the consensus algorithm used.

Historically, the average confirmation time for a Bitcoin transaction has been around 10 minutes, while Litecoin boasts an average confirmation time of 2.5 minutes.

While Bitcoin uses the longstanding SHA-256 consensus algorithm, Litecoin uses a relatively new algorithm called Scrypt. The main difference in these algorithms is in the mining of coins. Bitcoin miners can use dedicated and efficient mining machines called ASICs, while Litecoin can't be mined with ASICs, encouraging mining with traditional CPUs and GPUs, making mining more accessible.

Interesting facts:

Litecoin is called the silver to Bitcoin's gold.

At the end of 2017 Charlie Lee sold all of his LTC, as he was often accused of using his strong influence on social media to manipulate the price of LTC for his own benefit.

Like Bitcoin, Litecoin has also integrated the SegWit protocol, mainly because it allows the Lightning Network (LN) to be built on top of it.

Litecoin is able to handle higher transaction volumes. The network is planned to produce 84 million Litecoins, which are four times as many currency units as Bitcoin.

In February 2018, Litecoin had a hard-fork and Litecoin Cash was created. Litecoin Cash moved from the Scrypt algorithm back to SHA-256 algorithm, and as a result, the founders expect Litecoin Cash to become faster than the original Litecoin in the future.

Whitepaper: As Litecoin started off as a clone of Bitcoin, they haven't written a whitepaper
Website: https://litecoin.org/
Coinmarketcap: https://coinmarketcap.com/currencies/litecoin

NEO [NEO]

NEO is a blockchain platform and cryptocurrency which enables the development of digital assets and smart contracts. The project was founded by Da Hongfei in 2014 in China. The project was initially named AntShares, but later it was renamed to NEO.

NEO is quite similar to Ethereum. Both of them strive to create an ecosystem of decentralized applications (DApps), ICOs and smart contracts. But while, Ethereum has been around for some time and has already established itself, NEO is still relatively new and is still developing most of its aspects.

NEO uses a delegated Byzantine Fault Tolerance (dBFT) consensus mechanism, which compared to slower Proof-of-Work protocols that are used with Ethereum and Bitcoin, allows transaction speeds of up to 10,000 transactions per second (compared to Ethereum's 15 transactions per second).

NEO tokens can be used to produce GAS tokens which are used as the fuel of the platform, to pay for computation or deployment of smart contracts within the NEO network. This is similar to Ethereum's gas concept, but NEO has a separate GAS token for it while Ethereum doesn't.

Interesting facts:

NEO is often called "Chinese Ethereum".

NEO is partnered with a company called OnChain which has extensive experience in integrating blockchain with businesses.

While Ethereum only supports their own programming language – Solidity; NEO supports the most common programming languages around, including C, C++, C#, JavaScript, Java and Python.

NEO is essentially developing their platform to be quantum computer proof.

NEO is currently not a distributed blockchain, which means that, while it is decentralized, it is only operated on a few nodes, which are all controlled by NEO itself. But during 2018 they have promised to start distributing the network.

The cost of launching a smart contract on NEO is quite expensive – over $15,000 USD.

Whitepaper: http://docs.neo.org/en-us/

Website: https://neo.org/

Coinmarketcap: https://coinmarketcap.com/currencies/neo

Stellar [XLM]

Stellar is an open-source protocol for exchanging money founded by Jed McCaleb and Joyce Kim in early 2014. Stellar was initially based on Ripple systems, with the aim of redesigning the global economy for more inclusiveness. But citing the complexity of the system, Stellar later redesigned itself with a brand new system of its own. Both facilitate international payments, but do this in very different ways.

While Ripple is concentrating on banks and large financial institutions, Stellar is focused on the peer-to-peer aspect, and is mainly directed at companies and individuals. Like Ripple, Stellar offers many different ways to transact internationally, and almost instantly. Users have the ability to exchange fiat currencies instantly, eliminating the need for the money to go through many different banks to make the exchange. If no fiat based trades are available, users can use Lumens (Stellar's native cryptocurrency) to transact.

Ripple is a centralized cryptocurrency and a for-profit organization, while Stellar is a decentralized, non-profit organization.

Interesting facts:

The native asset of Stellar is called Lumens [XLM].

One of the major partners with Stellar is IBM.

While Ripple was developed by ex-bankers and financial professionals, Stellar was built by start-up veterans, like WordPress founder Matt Mullenweg and Y-Combinator President Sam Altman.

Jeb McCaleb, co-founder of Stellar, and also a co-founder of Ripple, was banished from Ripple before creating Stellar, but he still receives payments from the company.

Whitepaper: https://www.stellar.org/papers/stellar-consensus-protocol.pdf

Website: https://stellar.org

Coinmarketcap: https://coinmarketcap.com/currencies/stellar

Monero [XMR]

Monero is an open-source cryptocurrency created in April 2014 that focuses on privacy and decentralization. Monero aims to improve on existing cryptocurrency design by obscuring the sender, the recipient and the amount of every transaction made, as well as making the mining process more equal.

Unlike many cryptocurrencies that are derivatives of Bitcoin, Monero is based on the CryptoNight Proof-of-Work hash algorithm and uses different ways to make the currency as anonymous as possible.

For example, Ring Signatures combine many different senders' addresses together when the transactions are written into the ledger, which makes it incredibly difficult to trace the origin of the transaction. Monero also uses stealth addresses, which means that for every new transaction, users generate a new address. Also, Monero uses Ring Confidential Transactions, which hide the amounts in each transaction. All of these aspects contribute to Monero's outstanding anonymity.

Monero's mining is designed to be ASIC-proof, meaning that wealthier miners can't purchase expensive and extremely efficient ASICs to mine more Monero. This makes mining Monero more accessible, equal to every participant and makes the mining more decentralized.

Interesting facts:

> Monero's focus on privacy has attracted many people who are interested in evading the law. Its egalitarian mining process is also used by hackers who embed mining code into websites and apps.

> Monero uses Ring Signatures, Stealth Addresses and Ring Confidential Transactions to provide its users with maximum privacy.

Whitepaper: https://getmonero.org/resources/research-lab/
Website: https://getmonero.org
Coinmarketcap: https://coinmarketcap.com/currencies/monero

EOS [EOS]

EOS is a blockchain-based, decentralized operating system, designed to support commercial-scale decentralized applications by providing all of the necessary core functionality, enabling businesses to build blockchain applications in a way similar to web-based applications.

One of the co-founders of EOS is Dan Laimer, who has previously developed BitShares, Steemit and invented the Delegated Proof-of-Stake consensus algorithm (which is used in both, BitShares and EOS).

Two promised features of EOS have really caught everyone's attention: the elimination of transaction fees, and scalability. They say it can process millions of transactions per second with asynchronous communication and parallel processing. High transaction costs and bad throughput are Ethereum's critical weaknesses, so these features make EOS a serious contender for the title of go-to blockchain development solution. But currently EOS is still mostly conceptual and its ICO was conducted on the Ethereum blockchain (ERC-20).

Interesting facts:

"EOS" is not an officially defined acronym, but the community has given it many different names such as "Ethereum On Steroids", "End Of Silence", "Endless Online Scaling", and even "EOS Operating System".

EOS distributed their tokens during their ongoing 341-day ICO, which had an entirely novel structure. The ICO was divided into 350 23-hour long windows. In every window 2,000,000 EOS tokens were distributed amongst investors at market price.

The first 5 days of EOS's ICO were done "traditionally", during which EOS raised around $185M in ETH.

Running an EOS node requires a Linux/OS X operating system.

Whitepaper: https://github.com/EOSIO/Documentation/blob/master/TechnicalWhitePaper.md
Website: https://eos.io
Coinmarketcap: https://coinmarketcap.com/currencies/eos

Dash [DASH]

Dash is a peer-to-peer open-source cryptocurrency like Bitcoin, acting as digital cash that can be sent without the need for middlemen like the bank. Dash was created by Evan Duffield and launched on the 18th of January, 2014 as a fork of Litecoin. The coin started off under the name XCoin, later to be renamed to Darkcoin, and was finally rebranded to Dash (derivative of "Digital" and "Cash").

Compared to Bitcoin, Dash offers cheaper transaction fees and faster transactions. Regular Dash transaction blocks are confirmed every 2.5 minutes (compared to Bitcoin's 10 minutes), but for a larger transaction fee Dash's InstantSend function allows users send funds instantly.

Dash has integrated the PrivateSend function that combines identical inputs from different users into a single transaction, which flows through several outputs, adding to Dash's anonymity and security.

It is also self-governing, allowing important updates and changes to be incorporated much faster, and a funding model which makes it possible to pay the developers who build and improve the system.

Interesting facts:

Dash is classified as a DAO (decentralized autonomous organization) because of its self-governance practice

Within the first 48 hours that the coin was created, around 1.9 million or approximately 10% of the total supply of the coins were mined. This mishap happened because of a bug within the difficulty parameters in the code when Litecoin was forked to create Dash. This problem was quickly fixed.

Dash uses a two-tier network. The first tier consists of regular miners who confirm the transactions, and the second tier consists of MasterNodes that perform InstantSend, PrivateSend and governance functions.

Running a MasterNode costs an initial payment of 1000 DASH.

Dash's partnership with Coinapult makes it possible to buy Dash with over 20 different fiat currencies.

Whitepaper: https://github.com/dashpay/dash/wiki/Whitepaper
Website: https://www.dash.org/
Coinmarketcap: https://coinmarketcap.com/currencies/dash

IOTA [MIOTA]

IOTA is a next generation public distributed ledger that, unlike other cryptocurrencies that utilize blockchain, uses a novel technological approach called the "Tangle". The Tangle is a new data structure based on a Directed Acyclic Graph (DAG).

IOTA doesn't have Blocks, Chains or Miners. To make an IOTA transaction one must validate two previous transactions. This makes it possible for IOTA to reach consensus while allowing near instant payments for no transaction fee.

IOTA is specially created for Internet of Things (IoT) devices. It makes it feasible for these internet connected devices to make micro-transactions themselves, creating a Machine-to-Machine economy, where, for example, your solar panel has the ability to sell electricity to your neighbor's light bulbs.

Eliminating mining and incorporating the Tangle makes IOTA endlessly scalable, as the more users there are, the faster and stronger the network becomes.

Interesting facts:

IOTA was founded in 2014 as a German non-profit organization.

IoT devices have been regarded as the 4th industrial revolution, as it opens up never before seen opportunities, and IOTA is positioning itself as a critical factor to make the IoT revolution happen. The Internet of things (IoT) is the network of physical devices, vehicles, home appliances and other items embedded with electronics, software, sensors, actuators, and connectivity which enables these objects to connect and exchange data [Wikipedia].

In November 2017, Microsoft's Blockchain specialist, Omkar Naik was quoted saying that Microsoft will partner with IOTA, which was later proven not to be the case.

In December of 2017 the price of IOTA skyrocketed from around $1 to $5 in a matter of a week, as IOTA announced partnerships with Samsung and Fujitsu.

Whitepaper: https://iota.org/IOTA_Whitepaper.pdf

Website: https://iota.org/

Coinmarketcap: https://coinmarketcap.com/currencies/iota

NEM [XEM]

The New Economy Movement (NEM) is an enterprise-grade solution created to power the impending blockchain economy, focused on creating a smart asset blockchain which could effectively work under heavy workloads. Originally NEM was intended to be a fork of NXT, but the community decided to go with a completely new code. The alpha release was launched on June 25, 2014 and the full version was launched on March 31, 2015.

NEM introduced many novel aspects to the world of blockchain, such as its Proof-of-Importance (POI) algorithm, multi-signature accounts and encrypted messaging.

NEM's Proof-of-Importance is similar to the Proof-of-Stake protocol. There are no miners in POI, instead there are harvesters, who are given an importance score based on the amount of NEM they hold and how much they contribute to the network.

NEM has two different blockchains; one is a public blockchain that can currently handle only around 2 transactions per second, and the other one is a private blockchain that can process up to 4000 transactions per second. The private blockchain, called Mijin, used for testing, but during 2018 NEM's public blockchain will have an update called "Catapult" that will introduce the speed of the private blockchain to the public chain, making it over 2000x's faster than the current version.

Interesting facts:

The idea behind NEM was started by a Bitcointalk forum user called UtopianFuture, who is keeping himself pseudonymous.

The launch of the currency was not a smooth road. People who held the NEMstake asset or signed up to the Bitcointalk forum to receive their coins did not receive them. Instead, the coins were kept by the developers.

To run a booted and synchronized node, a harvester must hold at least 10,000 NEM.

At the start of 2018, over $500 million in NEM was stolen from the Tokyo-based cryptocurrency exchange Coincheck.

Whitepapers and documents: https://docs.nem.io/en
Website: https://nem.io/
Coinmarketcap: https://coinmarketcap.com/currencies/nem

Can Cryptocurrency be Used in the Real World?

The natural habitat of cryptocurrencies is the internet. There are more and more online stores accepting cryptocurrencies as a payment method. In addition, an increasing number of physical stores have started to accept crypto, plus there are Bitcoin ATMs where you can withdraw BTC as the converted local currency or deposit your cash to convert it into Bitcoin. Above that, there are also cryptocurrency debit cards which can be used almost everywhere where regular debit cards are accepted.

Conclusion

The most popular function of the blockchain, cryptocurrencies, have garnered the mistaken reputation of being only used by criminals, while in reality they are meant for use by the general population at large. They are meant for everyone who likes fast transaction speeds, lower costs and improved security, plus they can also be used as investment vehicles.

Case Study #6

How Does the Ethereum Blockchain Work?

Ethereum is a blockchain-based, open-source, smart contract platform, meaning that while the early cryptocurrencies, like Bitcoin, acted only as a store of value that could be transacted with, Ethereum allows users to create smart contracts, issue their own tokens, and run decentralized apps (DApps), making it possible to do a lot more things on the blockchain than before.

Smart contracts are contracts running on the blockchain that execute themselves upon certain actions. You can compare smart contracts with vending machines. You insert some money into the vending machine, which triggers the ability to choose a beverage, and your choice triggers the machine to release your drink. Smart contracts work similarly but instead of granting you a refreshing drink, they execute actions and code on the blockchain allowing users to create different decentralized applications, or smart contracts.

These applications consist of different smart contracts working in harmony, which are executed by the Ethereum Virtual Machine (EVM). It takes the code from these applications and broadcasts it to the miners who run these codes.

Miners keep the network running, run the code, and allow users to do all of these things on the Ethereum blockchain. They have to be incentivised by something so that they will be motivated to use their computing power to keep their mining operations up. And this is where gas comes in.

What is gas?

Sending gas is a sacrificial ritual to the Ethereum gods (otherwise known as miners) who make it possible for mere mortals to use the magical powers of the Ethereum blockchain. Or in other words, it is the transaction fee which is paid to the miners in exchange for their computing power that keeps the network running and allows users to make transactions. Gas is the thing that makes it profitable for miners to use their computing power to mine. But why does Ethereum use gas instead of ETH? Is this some sort of an elaborate joke made by the Ethereum team to make things unnecessarily difficult?

Actually, it is not a joke and there is a very simple explanation for this. While the price of ETH fluctuates quite drastically almost every day, the cost of computing remains constant. If the transaction fee was a certain amount of ETH, it would mean: a) that the network would constantly have to adjust to the new price of ETH, which would be inefficient; b) if the network doesn't adjust to the new price, then during price drops, mining would become unprofitable and the network would have a lot less (if any) miners. On the other hand, if the price increases drastically, transacting on Ethereum would become too expensive.

To solve this problem Ethereum uses gas. Gas is not a separate token that is used to pay the fee, instead, it is paid in ETH, but is calculated by multiplying gas limit and gas price. This disconnects the price of ETH from the fee that's paid to the miners, which keeps the mining operations profitable to miners at all times and keeps the network stable.

Both gas limit and gas price can be changed when making a transaction, so why would anyone want to spend more money on a transaction if it's not mandatory?

Gas Price

Gas price is the value of one unit of gas. So, if anyone can change the gas price, why would someone want to increase it, when they can just keep it low?

When someone makes a transaction on the Ethereum blockchain (it is similar in almost all blockchains), the transaction is first checked to confirm that the account actually has enough funds to make such a transaction. If everything is OK, the transaction is added to a pool that contains all of the unmined transactions (in the senders perspective, this is where your transaction waits if you see that it is "pending").

When miners put together the blocks they are mining, they fill them with the transactions that are in this pool. All of these transactions have gas attached to them which will be given to the miners if they include these transactions to their blocks. In the process of adding transactions to their blocks, miners prioritize transactions with higher gas prices, as these are more profitable to them.

To make a long story short, gas price determines how quickly your transaction is included in a block. A higher gas prices ensures a faster transaction, while a lower gas price saves you some money, but is added to a block at a slower rate. At the time of writing, the standard gas price is around 4 Gwei (0.000000004 ETH), which will get your transaction confirmed in less than 5 minutes. If you're in a hurry, setting your gas price at 25 Gwei will get your transaction confirmed in less than 2 minutes, but if time is not of the essence, you can set your gas price lower. These gas prices can be checked **online.**

Miners

When miners set up their mining operations they create a set of rules for it. They can define the minimum gas price of transactions that they'll add to their blocks. Setting a threshold for the gas price allows miners to only concentrate on profitable transactions, maximizing their profits. There's no point in mining transactions that result in a low profit or in a loss.

Gas Limit

Gas limit is the maximum amount of gas you are willing to spend on a transaction.

Smart contracts run until they are either completed or when they run out of gas. If there wouldn't be a gas limit, then there would be nothing that would stop a contract with an error for running forever.

Gas limit is there to protect the network from DDoS attacks, making sure that the network isn't spammed with a bunch of looping contracts that waste resources and clog up the network, and it also avoids situations where a contract with an error keeps running forever, devouring the creator's valuable resources.

All of the functions that make up smart contracts have a set amount of gas they use, which are written down in the Ethereum yellow paper. For example, a simple ETH transaction between two wallets uses 21,000 gas.

If someone tries to create a transaction with an insufficient gas limit, then the transaction fails due to an "out of gas" error and the funds are not sent. While the funds will not leave the wallet, the gas attached to the transaction is given to the miners regardless whether the transaction succeeds or not. Miners still had to spend their computing power to process your failed transaction.

Example

Now let's quickly illustrate how gas is calculated and spent.

If you want to send 1 ETH to your friend, you would have to pay an additional 21,000 (gas limit for an ETH transaction) x 0.000000004 ETH (or 4 Gwei, the standard gas price) = 0.000084 ETH for gas.

If you want to make sure that the transaction is completed as soon as possible you might want to increase the gas price to make it more attractive to the miners to add it to their blocks. Setting your gas price at 25 Gwei means that your transaction gets completed in less than 2 minutes and you'll have to pay 21,000 x 0.000000025 ETH = 0.000525 ETH.

If you would have set the gas limit at 20,000 and kept the gas price the same, your 1 ETH would not reach your friend, but the 20,000 x 0.000000004 ETH = 0.00008 ETH will still be paid to the miners.

If you would have set your gas limit at 30,000 instead and kept the gas price the same, your 1 ETH will reach your friend, 21,000 x 0.000000004 ETH = 0.000084 ETH will be given to the miners, but the remaining 9,000 x 0.000000004 ETH = 0.000036 ETH will be refunded to you.

Why Does the Ethereum Network Get Clogged Up?

Like we said before, all of the unmined/pending transactions are in a pool, waiting for their time to be added to blocks. During normal times everything works just fine, and the amount of new transactions being broadcast to the pool is around the same as the number of transactions getting mined and added into blocks.

But during hectic periods, like ICOs, or when someone creates an app that uses a lot of micro-transactions, like CryptoKitties, then the network can clog up quite fast. This is because the amount of transactions entering the mining pool exceeds the number of transactions getting mined. It is like a pool at a waterpark, where there are hundreds of people sliding down the waterslide, and the pool only has one ladder out - when the pool gets quickly filled with people, they cannot exit the pool with speed.

This is one of the main problems with current blockchain platforms that needs to be solved before this technology becomes viable for everyday use. For example, Status ICO created delays in the network lasting for hours, and even days, and Cryptokitties quickly filled up the mining pool, causing over 10,000 pending transactions within a couple of days after going live.

To get a transaction mined during busy times, there are mainly two ways. One way is to increase your gas price so that the miners are incentivised to include your transactions to their blocks first and foremost. And the other is for the miners to increase their block gas limit, which means that more transactions will fit into the blocks. Block gas limit is the maximum amount of gas that can be included in a block. It is similar to the 1MB Bitcoin block size, but since Ethereum can do a lot more than Bitcoin, measuring the blocks in terms of kilobytes doesn't work. Some contracts that have a small size could run forever and waste a lot of resources. This is why Ethereum uses block gas limit instead of a certain block size limit.

Participating in an ICO

One of the most popular use cases for Ethereum is issuing your own token and launching an ICO. Tokens created on Ethereum are called ERC20 tokens. These tokens, as well as their ICOs, are based on Ethereum's smart contracts.

As mentioned before, the amount of gas used for a transaction depends on the amount of code in the contract. While regular ETH transactions use a constant 21,000 gas, token transactions can range anywhere from 50,000 to 200,000 or even more gas.

ICOs are usually time-bound, meaning that there's a certain timeframe when these tokens can be purchased. And since these token transactions tend to clog up the Ethereum network, it is often suggested to use a higher gas price. All of the information about the gas limit and gas price is usually provided by the ICO creator when announcing the launch of the ICO.

If you set your gas limit too low when purchasing ICO tokens, this can result in an "out of gas" error and you'll lose the transaction fee, or if you don't have a high enough gas price, your transaction could take a long time before getting confirmed.

Conclusion

Gas is the transaction fee that is paid to the miners in exchange for their computing power, which keeps the network running, processes data, runs code and validates transactions.

Gas is not a separate token, it is paid in ETH.

The transaction fees are presented in gas instead of ETH because while the price of computing remains constant, the price of ETH fluctuates quite a bit. Disconnecting the price of ETH from the cost of computing creates more stability and flexibility.

Transaction fee = gas limit x gas price.

Gas price is the value of one unit of gas.

Higher gas price ensures that your transaction is prioritized by the miners and processed faster.

Lower gas price will save you some money, but your transaction gets mined slower.

Gas limit is the amount of gas you are willing to spend on a transaction. Ethereum's smart contracts consist of different functions that use a predetermined amount of gas for running and everyone who wants to transact with these contracts has to provide the sufficient amount of gas to get the transaction completed.

If the gas limit is set too low, then the transaction fails due to "out of gas" error.

If the gas limit is set higher than necessary, then the transaction is completed and the remaining, unused gas is refunded to the sender.

During hectic periods, like such as ICOs or when there're a lot of micro-transactions (Cryptokitties), then the Ethereum network can get clogged up and create delays lasting for hours or even days. Increasing your gas price to take into account the network congestion will get your transaction completed faster.

ICOs are different from regular ETH transactions. They use more functions than regular transactions and thus require more gas to run. These amounts are usually presented by the creator of the ICO. Due to increased amounts of transactions, it is also suggested to increase the gas price to ensure a faster confirmation time.

Case Study #7

What is SegWit?

Problem With the Current System

Currently, the block size of Bitcoin is limited to 1MB. This size was fine in the beginning, where only a handful of people used BTC to make transactions. Now that the popularity of Bitcoin has grown exponentially, this block size is not enough.

Due to the combination of limited space inside the blocks and the overwhelming amount of pending transactions waiting to be added into blocks, it makes the system slow and more expensive. All of the pending transactions don't fit into the blocks, so miners can only add some of them into blocks that get added to the blockchain. This means that some transactions take hours, or even days, to be validated.

It also creates an incentive to increase the transaction fees. Because miners have to pick a handful of transactions that they'll add into their blocks, they tend to pick the ones with the highest transaction

How Can We Solve it?

In order to solve this problem, there are two solutions. One of them is the use of Segregated Witness (SegWit) and the other is simply increasing the block size.

What Does SegWit Mean?

SegWit is an optimization proposed by Pieter Wuille, a Bitcoin Core developer. This optimization increases the amount of transactions that fit into blocks without changing the block size. It takes one of the most size-heavy parts of the transactions, the signatures (also called "witnesses", hence the name segregated witness, or 'separated signature'), and puts them at the bottom of the block. This data is called witness data, and is sometimes referred to as extended blocks.

In order to keep the SegWit update a soft-fork, meaning that nodes don't necessarily have to update their software, the optimization had to find a way to still satisfy the rule of 1MB block size.

The way SegWit deals with it is that "legacy" nodes (the nodes that run the traditional Bitcoin protocol without the SegWit update) receive blocks without the witness data, while updated nodes receive the blocks with the witness data. This means that the size of the blocks sent to legacy nodes are still 1MB or below, while containing more transactions as the blocks don't contain the signatures, allowing more transactions to be fit into blocks.

The only limitation with this is that the legacy nodes can't validate SegWit blocks as validation requires the witness data, which they don't have. This also means that legacy nodes will only receive blocks with SegWit transactions once the blocks have been validated by the SegWit nodes.

While blocks without the witness data that are sent to legacy nodes are kept at 1MB or lower, the SegWit blocks that have the witness data can theoretically reach up to 4MB, but the actual size depends on the network and is more likely to be around 2MB.

What Does Increasing the Blocksize Mean?

This implies changing the protocol, increasing the block size limit from 1MB to, let's say, 2MB. This means that the new blocks can contain twice as many transactions than they did previously.

SegWit2x

A compromise was made in the 23rd of May, 2017 and it is known as the New York Agreement. This compromise was to implement the SegWit soft-fork as well as increase the block size limit from 1MB to 2MB.

This is called SegWit2x and this agreement was signed by the 58 companies that control around 83% of the hashing power. The objective of SegWit2x was not to create two separate Bitcoins like the Bitcoin Cash and Bitcoin Gold hard-forks did, but to make the SegWit2x Bitcoin the primary Bitcoin, bearing the legendary symbol of BTC.

The SegWit optimization was incorporated into Bitcoin as of August 2017, but the Segwit2x (hard-fork) would have created two separate branches of Bitcoin, and the community would have been split forever. Although the developers of SegWit2x know that 1MB block size is not enough, but they understand that keeping the community together is even more important. Because of this, the hard-fork was cancelled on November 8, 2017.

Although the hard-fork was cancelled, the SegWit protocol is here to stay, making way to incorporate side chain solutions like the Lightning Network to Bitcoin. The Lightning Network works by moving some transactions off the main blockchain to side chains. This solution allows the creation of a payment channel off the blockchain to happen between two people. This makes transactions faster and cheaper as they won't exhaust the main blockchain. This also makes it much more scalable and more versatile, by making micropayments feasible. When there happens to be a dispute, the transactions can be moved back to the main blockchain and settled there by the verifying network.

Smart Contracts

What are Smart Contracts?

Smart contracts are contracts that work on blockchain technology. In its essence, a smart contract is a software program that contains an "If-This-Then-That" function, meaning if something happens on a smart contract, it triggers another action.

The creator of smart contracts, Nick Szabo, illustrated the idea of the "If-This-Then-That" function with the good old vending machine. If you put some money in the machine and choose a product it makes the machine release the chosen product. If you don't put enough money in the machine, then the machine won't release the product and you can get your money back or add to it to make the purchase. Basically, once you do something, another action follows.

Concept

Smart contracts are programs that trigger certain actions once they are acted upon, or not. This idea is nothing new – contracts have been around for a long time and automation is also nothing revolutionary. Smart contracts tie both of them together and put them onto the blockchain.

With regular contracts, you have to rely on third-parties in order for them to work. For example, when transferring money, you have to trust that the bank does, in fact, send the money. You also have to trust that the bank doesn't randomly take your money away from your account. With documents, you have to trust a lawyer or a notary to validate them. And you have to trust that your doctor won't share your medical records with anybody.

With the integration of blockchain technology, smart contracts eliminate the need for having third-parties. Instead of one central server that processes the information, holds the data and contracts, there are a lot of computers around the world, which all hold and validate the data. This data is put into blocks and these blocks are stored in a chronological order, creating the blockchain. Once a smart contract is put into a block and the block is added to the blockchain, it is there permanently and unalterably. These blocks are also completely public and transparent, meaning every participant can validate these contracts.

With removing the middlemen from the equation, we eliminate the need of having to rely on trust. In addition, when middlemen are cut out from the equation, the cost of creating a contract decreases and the possibility of having your information or money stolen greatly decreases.

Benefits of Smart Contracts

Automation, trust, speed – since no third-parties are involved, the processes are acted upon faster and automatically. The information does not have to go through different people, who would need to do extensive paperwork. Instead it is acted upon instantly.

Backup – the fact that all of the information and contracts are stored not in a centralized server that could crash, but in a network of computers, makes it impossible to lose all of your data. When one of the computers crashes, nothing happens to the contract, because it is still stored in all of the other computers within the network.

Security – the information about the contract is held on the blockchain. If a hacker wants to modify the data presented in the contract, he would have to hack all of the computers in the network at the same time and rework the entire network, which is quite impossible.

Precision – the contracts are run by computers who don't make human errors.

Example

To illustrate how smart contracts can be used in the real world, let's use an example.

Imagine you want to send your friend Jake a cake for his birthday, but you want to be absolutely sure that during the delivery process no-one eats the delicious cake. Traditionally you would have to rely on trust and hope that the delivery company's employees are well-fed and won't eat the cake.

But with the new technology, you can create a smart contract, and send the money for the delivery to that contract. This contract is broadcast to the network of computers, which confirm that the transaction has been made and the delivery company is notified. The delivery company makes the delivery and Jake signs the contract, confirming that the cake has been received without having any bites taken out of it. This signature releases the payment you made and is sent to the delivery company.

This example shows how smart contracts can work as an Escrow service and how it motivates both parties to deliver on their end, without having to rely on blind trust, while also making the process faster, cheaper and more secure.

Uses for Smart Contracts

Voting

One of the best use cases for smart contracts is the voting process. Governments can create a smart contract so that instead of citizens waiting in lines to cast their vote, they can cast their vote via their phones or computers. Every voter could be given an ID, which would not be related to their true identity, keeping them anonymous. They can then cast their vote to the contract and the network behind the smart contract would confirm that the person hasn't voted before, and that the vote hasn't been corrupted. This would drastically decrease the likelihood of fraud, while also making voting more popular amongst people because it only takes a few taps on the screen to cast a vote.

Record Keeping

Another thing that can be improved upon is record keeping. You can be the boss of your personal information by being able to give and remove access to your data through smart contracts. You can give your doctor access to your medical records, but she won't be able to give access to anyone without it being allowed by you. If you decide to switch your doctor, you can remove the old doctor's access to your data. This way you can be sure that your information isn't misused.

Banking

Of course there is banking. Like we mentioned before, currently, many people have to trust their money to a bank. You have to hope that the bank does not misplace, mismanage or steal your money, and that the transactions you make do in fact reach the right person. Plus, you have to trust that the bank's servers don't get hacked.

Instead of using banks, people can move their account information and balance to the blockchain. Everyone on the network would have the ability to see how much money an account has, but at the same time, all of the other information would be kept anonymous, keeping their identity safe. When making a transaction, all of the computers on the blockchain validate whether the account has enough funds to make this payment. Once confirmed the transaction is made and the blockchain is updated.

When Bob, who has €100 on his balance, wants to send €25 to Lisa, the transaction is broadcast to the network. All of the computers in the network check whether Bob has enough money to send €25. Once it is confirmed that the money was sent to Lisa, the information is updated. Now Bob has €75 on his balance and Lisa has €25 more than before. Once the information is updated it cannot be changed. In this process there are no banks involved, and all of the validation is done by the network. This ensures the security of your money, and makes the whole process cheaper.

These are just some examples where the use of smart contracts has a great advantage over the traditional system of contracts.

Conclusion

In short, smart contracts are contracts that are stored on the blockchain instead of a central database. This makes the contracts more reliable, secure and transparent. It also eliminates middlemen from the equation, who could alter and manipulate the information in the contract and above that, charge high fees for their services. Smart contracts create automated systems, which are faster and don't make human errors.

Cryptography

Introduction

One of the main tools used to make blockchains secure is called cryptography. Cryptography is the practice of secret communication in the presence of third parties. It uses mathematical algorithms to encrypt information in a way that resembles complete nonsense, and normally is represented as a jumble of letters and numbers. To decipher this 'nonsense' you will need to use a specific key.

You can think of encryption as locking information in an indestructible box with a really complex lock. To open the box and see the information inside, you will need the corresponding, or matching, key. Without the right key, you have no means of opening the box. The lock on the box is so complex that it would take the most talented lock picker thousands or even millions of years to pick the lock. But if you have the right key, then you can open it in seconds.

One simple example of cryptography is the use of secret letters. Remember when you were just a small child and wanted to send your friend a message that could only be read by him? In order to do that, you would think up a secret language that only the two of you could understand. For example, you may have used numbers instead of letters, or switched up certain letters (A=1, B=2, C=3 etc.). This is cryptography in its simpler form.

> **Fun fact:** Cryptography has been around for a long time. The first known case of cryptography was in 1900 BC in Ancient Egypt. This encryption wasn't very difficult nor functional, instead, it was used for entertainment.

Uses

Cryptographic practices are used daily, from sending sensitive information between you and your friend to planning military tactics. For example, Julius Caesar used encrypted messages to send communications to his generals (his encryption of choice is now known as the Caesar Cipher, shifting the letters in the alphabet by 3, so A=D, B=E, C=F, and so on), and you may have heard about the Enigma machine, which was used in World War II.

Cryptography is also a part of our everyday activities. For example, our emails and bank accounts are encrypted to make sure that no-one can simply hack into them. In addition, every time you visit a website that starts with "https://", it means that the connection to the website is encrypted and more secure.

How it works

Cryptography is in use everywhere, every day, such as with your Smart Phone, online bank account and email. But how does it work?

Cryptography uses mathematical algorithms to scramble data so it's unreadable by unintended parties. There are many different types of cryptography and each type has its own characteristics. The main differences are how the encryptions are done, the speed of encryption, and their security, but all of them have the same purpose – to secure and hide data.

Encryptions and Keys

Encryption algorithms work with keys to secure data that has been encrypted. These keys give permission to users to encrypt and decrypt data. Keys are usually very long numbers which are combined with the data one wants to hide and then encrypted. To decrypt that   data, one needs to have   the respective key.

The strength of the encryption is relative to the key size. The key size is measured in bits – the more bits a key has, the stronger the encryption. There are different types of encryptions, which use different types of keys.

Symmetrical Cryptography – Conventional Keys

The first type of cryptography is called symmetrical cryptography because it uses just one key. This key can be used for both encryption and decryption. In order for this method to work, you must share the key with people you want to exchange messages with.

To illustrate, you and Judy want to send each other personal messages that you don't want anybody else to see. You decide to use symmetrical cryptography. You encrypt your message and send it to Judy. You also send Judy the key used to encrypt the data, so she can decrypt it. It's basically like a box that has multiple copies of the key for both opening and locking the box.

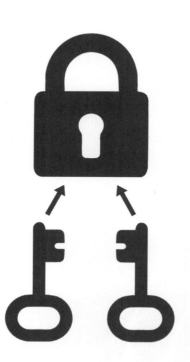

This system works but there is a problem. What if someone else, like Jack, happens to get his hands on a copy of this key? Maybe he saw the key you sent to Judy, and created a duplicate of it, and now has access to these messages.

Asymmetrical Cryptography – Public and Private Keys

To solve this problem you could use asymmetrical cryptography, which uses two separate keys for locking and unlocking the data. These keys are called public and private keys.

This method can be used to solve the problem we talked about with the conventional keys, as it removes the need for sharing one key that can both open and close the lock.

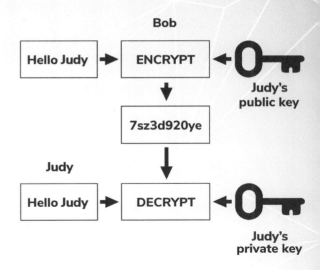

Now that you are smarter, you decide to use asymmetrical encryption to send your message to Judy. You take Judy's public key and use it to encrypt your message, and then send it to Judy. Judy receives the encrypted message, takes her private key and decrypts the message without any trouble. Now when Jack gets his hands on this encrypted message, he has no means of opening the encryption without knowing Judy's private key. As long as Judy doesn't share her private key, the message is safe from prying eyes.

Now, why would you use your private key to encrypt data if it can be decrypted by anyone with your public key? One reason is that it can act as a digital signature for authentication. It serves the same purpose as the handwritten signature while being almost impossible to counterfeit.

Let's say you want to sell your car to Jim. For that, you create an invoice, send it to Jim and ask him to sign the bill to make things official. Jim uses his private key to encrypt the invoice. Now everyone can take Jim's public key and verify that this was, in fact, Jim that signed/encrypted the document.

If for some reason, after the document is signed and you have given the car keys to Jim, he starts arguing that he hasn't received any document that says that he has to pay you anything for the car, you can simply take Jim's public key and validate that Jim has signed the bill of sale, or contract.

Hashing

One other cryptographic function related to blockchain is called hashing. Hashing is a kind of cryptography. The information stored in the blocks is secured and stored as a big string of numbers called a hash or hash value, which can never be changed. Hashing is a way to take information and make a secret code. You cannot reverse them.

Hashing is the way that information in blocks is made safe and secure. You cannot decrypt, or decode, hashes.

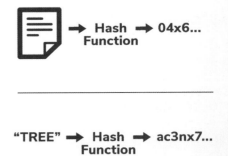

The hashing function takes an input and generates an output of certain length.

For example, you can take this entire chapter on one hand and the word "tree" on the other hand, put them through the hash function, and both of them could result in a hash of 64 characters (the amount of characters depends on the algorithm used). This characteristic is used to greatly decrease the size of data that is sent via the blockchain.

Another characteristic of the hash function is that even the smallest change in the input changes the output drastically. The words "apple" and "Apple" result in two completely different hashes. This is extremely useful for determining whether a document has been altered without knowing the contents of it.

For example, if the ownership document for your house is hashed and put onto the blockchain, then everyone can easily validate this document as true and unaltered.

Now let's say Rob suddenly decides that he is the owner of your house, and somehow puts his name on the ownership document for your house. This means that the altered document will produce a completely different hash, and when it is compared with the original document's hash, they will not match, making it obvious that Rob's document is corrupted. The blockchain network sees this difference easily and can discard the false document, leaving Rob without the right to your house.

HASH FUNCTION ONE WAY

Hash functions are also one-way functions, meaning that an output can be easily generated from an input, but it is impossible to do the other way around. Once something is hashed, the only way to reveal the input would be to start guessing. This, as you might think, is not a very easy nor time efficient task, and this is the exact reason why information on the blockchain in the form of hashes is so secure.

What's the Difference Between Hashing and Encryption?

The main difference is that while they both use cryptography to lock and hide data, encrypted messages can be easily decrypted with certain keys, while hashes are irreversible.

Multiset or Multi Signature Cryptography

Multi Signature Cryptography means that instead of one public and one private key, you can have multiple sets of keys. This creates many new opportunities in terms of security, accessibility and flexibility.

Two factor authentication - You can create 2 sets of private keys that both have to be used to access your cryptocurrency wallet. Storing these keys on separate devices creates a simple two factor authentication process – to log into your wallet you will have to approve the sign in from both of these devices. If have this process set in place, then you can rest assured that no one can take money from your wallet if you leave your computer open at work.

Shared account – Similar to the last point, you can create 2 sets of keys, but instead of holding them to yourself, you can give one set to a friend, family member or a business partner. For example you can have one shared account with your business partner, but if someone wants to use the company's resources they will need approval from the other person.

Secure and backed up – One of the problems with the above two examples is that if one private key is lost, then you will no longer have access to the account. To solve this you could create 3 sets of keys, but the account only requires 2 out of these 3 to access. You can store one set on your laptop, one on your phone and one on a piece of paper or memory stick inside a safe. You will have all of the benefits of two factor authentication, but if you lose one of these keys, for example from your phone, then you can still access your account with the two remaining keys (from your laptop and your safe).

Escrow – One of the most popular use cases for multisig is for escrow accounts. You can create 3 keys for an account from which 2 are required to access it. When purchasing a product, you can give one of these keys to the merchant, the second one to a trusted third party (escrow agent or an attorney), and you'll keep the third one. When making a purchase you'll send your money to the escrow account from where it is released to the merchant once the product arrives – both you and the merchant use your keys and release the funds. If there's a problem and the package doesn't arrive, then you won't use your key to release the funds and neither does the third party until the situation is resolved.

Hybrid Cryptography

Different kinds of cryptographic functions can also be used together to produce certain results.

For example, as previously explained, you can hash the ownership document of your house and before storing it on the blockchain, you can encrypt it with your private key, authenticating that this is the hash of the correct document. Everyone can verify that you have signed the document and also when Rob comes along and decides to mess with the original document, the corrupted document can easily be identified and discarded. And because of hashing, it can all be done without revealing the details presented in the document.

It is also possible to use both symmetrical and asymmetrical cryptography to secure a document. Asymmetrical cryptography offers far better security and flexibility than symmetrical cryptography, but it also takes a lot more time to encrypt something. Symmetrical encryption on the other hand is fast, but not as secure.

For example, when sending a delicate and lengthy message, you can seal the message symmetrically with the conventional key. This saves you quite a bit of time, as it is much faster than asymmetric cryptography.

Now, to create an extra layer of security around it, you take the conventional key and you encrypt it with the recipient's public key (asymmetrical cryptography). Because the conventional key is a lot shorter than your entire message, it will not take so much time to encrypt it as would encrypting the whole message.

Once secured, you can send both the encrypted message as well as the encrypted conventional key to the recipient. The recipient would use their private key to decrypt the conventional key, and then use the conventional key to decrypt the message.

By using hybrid cryptography in conjunction with smart contracts, we can create a better, more secure voting system. It could make voting more popular and eliminate corruption. In this system, people can cast their vote on the internet, by logging into their voting account and making their choice. Their vote would be hashed, signed with their private key and stored on the blockchain. To verify that the vote has not been altered with, the blockchain community can check whether the person who cast the vote actually signed the vote.

This would happen by using this person's public key to decrypt the vote. If the community is able to decrypt the vote with the person's public key, then they have signed it and it is valid. If they cannot decrypt the vote with the person's public key, then it has not been signed and is not valid. Hashing ensures that once the community verifies the vote, they will not be able to see the actual contents of the vote, but the hash. This allows people to confirm whether the vote has been altered in any way or not by comparing the signed hash to the hash that was initially stored on the blockchain. If the hashes match, then everything is as it should be. If not, then the vote has been altered and corrupted.

Conclusion

The use of cryptography with blockchain technology results in unbelievable security, and since all of these different cryptographic practices can be combined, they can be made to fit almost every situation. You can send private information, authenticate documents, prove ownership and easily verify if data has been altered, or not.

ITOs and ICOs

What are ITOs/ICOs?

If you have been keeping track of the news surrounding blockchain and cryptocurrencies, you probably have heard about ITOs or ICOs. These stand for Initial Token Offering (ITO) and Initial Coin Offering (ICO). Although we explained the difference between coins and tokens, in this chapter we are going to use them as synonyms.

ITOs/ICOs are basically the IPOs (Initial Public Offerings) of the blockchain world. Companies use them to receive funding for their venture, before they have released any products or when they want to create a new line of products, but don't have the necessary funding to do them without help. You can think of them like crowdfunding projects, where people invest their money into the company, through the blockchain.

The company creates a token and sells it to investors. With the money they receive from the investors they make their plan a reality. Investors buy tokens because they see potential in the project and are motivated by the potentially high return on investment, passive income and/or receiving the planned product.

For example, your friend Kate has a brilliant plan for an awesome product, but she doesn't have enough money to create it. She creates a solid business plan and launches an ICO. You decide to lend a helping hand and buy €100 worth of her tokens. Your other friend Jacob also helps Kate out and buys €10 worth of tokens, and so do many other people. Kate receives enough money to make her vision a reality. After a year, she launches the product. You, your friend Jacob, and the other investors get the product for free, and a few months after the product launch, her company is a success and the price of her tokens has risen significantly. Your €100 investment is now worth €1000, and Jacob's tokens are worth €100 instead of €10. Kate got the opportunity to realize her vision and create her dream company, while you, Jacob, and other investors increased their investment significantly.

Why are Some Countries Banning ITOs/ICOs?

Now if these ITOs/ICOs are such win-win situations, then why are some countries banning them?

Well, not all of the people who launch ITOs and ICOs are good people - there are a small handful of individuals who have penetrated this space and do not have the public's best interests at heart. Some dubious individuals have noticed they can create an ITO/ICO, receive the money, and run away with it. This is because ITOs/ICOs run on the blockchain and there are no universal authorities who control this space - yet.

There is no authorized body to determine whether the creator of an ITO/ICO is a solid person with a good credit rating, or owns a successful company and holds an impressive track record, and that they will deliver on their promises. The SEC in America and authorities in other countries are attempting to start this legislation process, and in China, ICOs were banned for an unspecified period of time starting from the end of 2017.

Since the blockchain provides people with anonymity and the money can't be tracked, then once someone runs off with the money, it is very difficult to get these funds back. While IPOs have certain rules and restrictions, ICOs/ITOs have no regulations. For these reasons, some countries are banning them in order to protect their citizens. If an ITO or ICO has escrow, meaning that all of the money raised during an ICO is kept secure by a third party and cannot be accessed until certain conditions are met by the company holding the ICO, then it is protecting investors, participants, advisors and the other staff who are vested into the ICO, alike. There are many companies who offer escrow services to ITOs and ICOs, making these crowdfunding ventures a more secure investment opportunity.

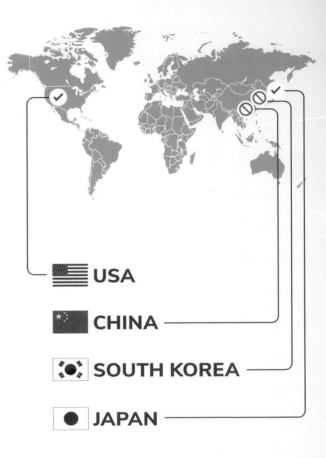

🇺🇸 **USA**

🇨🇳 **CHINA**

🇰🇷 **SOUTH KOREA**

🇯🇵 **JAPAN**

ITOs/ICOs have a lot of benefits aside from the drawbacks aforementioned, and most of the problems with ITOs/ICOs can be avoided with adequate research and knowledge about the ITO/ICO you are considering investing in. There are many legitimate investment opportunities out there, but you need to be well educated in the investment of your choice. People lose money mainly through cons and scams, and this is a problem which arises around any investment opportunity. Being educated on ITOs and ICOs, and crypto in general, will make you less vulnerable.

Conclusion

In conclusion, ITOs/ICOs provide blockchain companies with the opportunity to acquire funds to make their vision a reality, to create a new product, or to scale up their business. They can also bring a true opportunity to investors, and while they are condemned by some people as being scams, in reality, adequate knowledge and due diligence by ITO/ICO participants would have stopped many people from being taken advantage of by the truly fraudulent ITOs/ICOs.

How to choose an ICO to invest in

There's no doubt that the ICO market is booming. New ICOs are created almost every day and enormous amounts of capital is raised with almost every campaign. This new method of raising funds has attracted a lot of new people to the field of cryptocurrencies, with the amount of ICOs launched increased from 30 in 2016 to 891 in 2017. This is an increase of nearly 30 times! And the money raised in 2017 exceeded a staggering $6 billion USD (yes, billion).

The Importance of Being Educated

This exponential increase easily indicates the growing popularity of cryptocurrencies and ICOs, but where there is money there are scammers.

The cryptocurrency, blockchain and ICO industries are is still relatively new and the vast majority has no idea what they are, how they work and what their purposes are. This has made it very easy for malicious people to take advantage of hopeful, but uneducated individuals. Apart from not having enough knowledge around the topic, a lot of people have become money-hungry because of the incredible ROI past ICOs have provided. This makes people invest their hard-earned money without doing any research beforehand, making them ideal targets to scammers.

There are studies which show that up to 80% of ICOs are scams, accounting for over a billion USD lost for good. While you could say that it was a quite good run for the con men, it most definitely was not the greatest time for the people who lost their money.

Funds Raised With ICOs in 2016 vs 2017

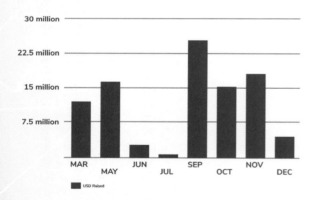

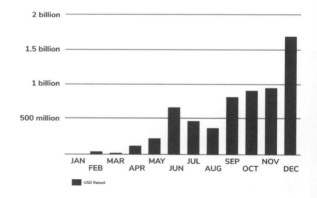

Funds Raised in 2016

Total funds:
$94,009,144

Number od ICOS:
30

Funds Raised in 2017

Total funds:
$6,026,914,791

Number od ICOS:
891

(Statistics from https://www.icodata.io/stats/2017)

ICOs by Category in 2018

- **Communications 21.8% ($969,953,600)**
- **Finance 18.0% ($799,701,539)**
- **Trading & Investing 13.9% ($617,237,136)**
- **Gaming & VR 9.4% ($416,049,113)**
- **Commerce & Advertising 6.2% ($275,965,500)**
- **Payments 5.4% ($240,025,329)**
- **Infrastructure 4.3% ($190,628,000)**
- **Machine Learning & AI 3.4% ($149,931,776)**
- **Energy & Utilities 2.3% ($101,500,000)**
- **Mining 2.3% ($100,000,000)**
- **Supply & Logistics 2.0% ($90,166,668)**
- **Drugs & Healthcare 2.0% ($89,178,011)**
- **Data Storage 1.6% ($69,000,000)**
- **Privacy & Security 1.5% ($66,793,221)**
- **Social Network 1.4% ($60,057,000)**
- **Data Analytics 1.3% ($57,017,078)**
- **Compliance & Security 0.9% ($39,544,101)**
- **Transport 0.7% ($29,500,000)**

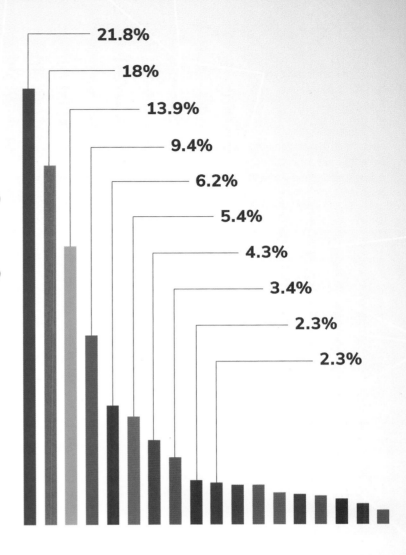

21.8%
18%
13.9%
9.4%
6.2%
5.4%
4.3%
3.4%
2.3%
2.3%

Scammers

This exponential increase easily indicates the growing popularity of cryptocurrencies and ICOs, but where there's money, there are scammers. Aside from motivated business people, looking to realize their dreams, this new emerging crowdfunding method has also attracted some dubious people.

A study done by Ernst and Young in 2017 on 372 ICOs uncovered that an astounding 10% of the $3.7B these campaigns raised was stolen or lost. This accounts to almost $400 million down the drain. While you could say that it was a quite good run for the scammers, it most definitely was not the greatest time for the people who lost their money.

Phishing and Fake ICOs

One of the tricks that scammers use with great success is called phishing, which means that they create fake ICO websites and campaigns to trick reckless investors to send their funds to the scammers' wallets. If investors are not careful they can easily fall for these kinds of schemes.

One of the most popular projects that scammers took advantage of was the ambitious Telegram ICO. While Telegram has cancelled their plan of launching an ICO, there were many fake Telegram ICO websites and ads circulating when it was being announced. Make sure you don't send your funds to a fake address by always checking if the website or advertising for an ICO comes from the real company that's launching the ICO. The first telltale sign of a fake website is the URL. Furthermore, legitimate ICOs will never ask you to give money through email or social media, and all contributions should go via their token order form, which is posted on their genuine ICO website.

It is also important to be aware of ICOs that have been wholly created as scams. There are many cases where someone writes a fancy whitepaper, launches an ICO, gathers all of the money that has been raised, and then runs off with it - leaving investors with empty hands and a really unpleasant experience.

To ensure you won't lose your money to a scammer, we put together some key points to look for prior taking part in an ICO. Feel free to print out this checklist and use it when researching ICOs which are of interest to you.

What to Look for Before Investing in an ICO:

The team

Is the information about the team public and transparent, or is the team anonymous?

While one of the purposes for blockchain technology is to eliminate the need for trust, and enable a certain level of anonymity, launching an ICO is not the place for that. Information about the team should be readily available and they should not be hiding information about themselves. Do extra research on the internet and find out as much as you can about the people involved. Don't depend on just looking at LinkedIn.

Who are in the team?

One of the most important things with any project is the team that is responsible for executing the plan. The solution isn't going to create itself, and there has to be a capable team behind the effort to make it happen.

What are their previous experiences and accomplishments?

The solution isn't going to create itself, and there has to be a capable team behind the ICO to make it successful. All of the team members should be well versed in the roles they have been assigned. If the team only consists of incompetent people with no experience, then the company will have a rather short lifespan. You should learn about the team members and see if any of them have done any successful projects in the past.

Why and how are they capable of realizing their goals?

This ties in with the last point. If the team has former experience in this field, they are more likely to succeed and not make stupid mistakes. The team should also cover all of the aspects of running a business. You can't have a successful project if team consists of only programmers or marketers, while no-one is looking after finances.

Are the team members competent in their roles in the company?

All of the team members should be well versed in the roles they have been assigned to. If the team only consists of incompetent people, then the company will have a rather short lifespan. Analyse the people, their position and if they are capable of filling that roles and completing all of the necessary tasks they might get.

Contact the team directly

It is one thing to read volumes of information on a website, but it is another thing to hear it from the source directly. You can get all of the answers to your questions about their ICO project from the team by contacting them via email or social media (their Linkedin profile, for instance).

Business plan, whitepaper and roadmap

Does their whitepaper explain everything about their project?

The whitepaper is there to provide all of the answers to questions potential investors and supporters might have. There should be detailed descriptions about how their product or service is filling a gap in the marketplace, how they are going to create the solution, an in-depth explanation of the product, an analysis of the marketplace and potential customers, roadmap, and more. The whitepaper should tell you everything.

Have they clearly described the need for their product, and how will they develop their product?

The product should solve real world issues and address a gap in the marketplace. There has to be a need for the solution as without demand, there will be no customers, and without sales, there will be no future for the company. The team should have a solid action plan about how they will actually create and technically develop their product. It's great if they have a vision, but this vision will need to be executed and without a concrete plan, it will be a huge mess and the progress will be glacially slow. A large percentage of ICOs fail and without a great plan, you can be sure that any ICO will fall into this category.

Why is their product/service useful for their customers? What problems will it solve?

The solution has to be useful to their customers, otherwise there's no point in starting a company in the first place. If the product doesn't solve any issues, then it's not likely to succeed. There has to be a place for the solution. If there are no customers then there won't be any sales, and if there are no sales, the company won't get any money and it will fail.

Is there anything like this ICO already out there?

If the ICO in question is just a copy of an already existing concept, then its chances of succeeding are diminished, unless the original concept was badly executed or there are major improvements and USPs (unique selling points) planned by the newer ICO project.

Do they have a ready prototype, or MVP (minimum viable product)?

If the company already has some sort of prototype or MVP, it indicates that the team is actually capable of creating the product they are raising funds for. Products in alpha or beta testing mean they are involving participants in gathering feedback about their product and can involve potential customers in the process of developing their product. This ensures that the solution they are creating is the one customers want and are willing to buy.

What is their revenue model?

Some ICOs future revenue strategies rely solely on the money they will collect during their ICO campaign. This strategy is not sustainable as once the money runs out, the company will most likely fail. This is sometimes indicated by unnecessarily large hard caps. If the business has a great product or service, then future revenue forecasts should not have to rely only on ICO money for their financial security.

Are there any gaps or problems with their ideas or business plan?

If you notice any pain points or find information is missing, analyze it and contact the team. They may have forgotten to add this information to their whitepaper or marketing materials, or they may have not considered these points.

Why are they doing an ICO?

What is the reason they are doing an ICO? Some companies launch an ICO because it is an easy way to quickly raise a large amount of money. And there is nothing wrong with this, but it is much better to invest in a company who has a plan to develop a new and more innovative product or transform their company to integrate use of the blockchain.

Is there a solid use case for their own cryptocurrency or is it just for fund raising?

There should be a proper use case for any ICO creating their token or coin. If they create a use for their cryptocurrency with regards to their project, for instance, allowing the token to act as a license fee or give priority access to the platform, then they have created what is known as a utility coin. If the only purpose for the coin is to sell them to investors in return for profits and dividends, or for other investment purposes, then the coin is classified as a security. If there is no real purpose for a coin or token, then the price of the coin will drop drastically on the exchanges after the ICO ends.

Do they have the support of any angel investors or VCs?

Another thing to look for is whether the project is already backed by angel investors or VCs. The current market encourages people to participate in ICOs for a quick profit, while not taking into consideration the actual business case and viability of the project. VCs and angel investors rarely make snap decisions with investments (if ever), and they analyze everything about an ICO before committing. The presence of VCs and angel investors shows there is something special about the project in question.

Have you done thorough research and your due diligence?

There are a lot of people who invest in ICOs for the sole reason being that someone on the internet suggested it. There are hundreds of YouTube videos which suggest different ICOs and coins to invest in, but provide very little reasoning behind the suggestion. For some people, they invest in a particular coin or token because it sounds "cool" to say that you are involved in the world of crypto and blockchain. There are many whitepapers and roadmaps out there which have been copied directly from other ICOs, which shows that there is a lack of professionalism or validity surrounding the project. If you want to keep your money, you should analyze the project as instructed above, and after understanding it, decide whether it is something you want to invest in.

Community

☐ **Are there people talking about the project and engaging in communities?**

If there are no conversations around the project, find out why there are none. Is it just that the project is not popular or is there another reason? Remember, there is no direct correlation between the number of users in Telegram and Social Media and the success of an ICO, as it is very easy to buy a community these days!

☐ **Is the team behind the project communicating with the community? Are they updating their community about their progress?**

Constant communication between the ICO and their supporters is important to show transparency and should include information about the progress of the ICO, solve supporters' problems and respond positively to valuable feedback that the community contributes.

☐ **Are the people in the community only praising the project?**

If the people who communicate on their channels only seem to promote the project and praise it no matter what, it could mean that these people are employed by this company, bots, or you might have actually found an interesting ICO.

And Finally

☐ **Are you ready to lose all of your investment?**

This might sound like a scary thought, but the reality is that nothing in this world is certain, and things are even less certain when dealing with crypto and blockchain, which is very volatile and still relatively new. There's always the possibility of losing it all, so you just need to invest with as much

Conclusion

It is easy to be attracted by the potential of a high ROI, and you might even get lucky a couple of times, but jumping in haphazardly is not a sustainable strategy. Use your common sense, do your own due diligence, and after following the checklist guideline to invest in an ICO, your chances of losing your money to scammers or con men will drastically decrease.

Transactions on the Blockchain

Introduction

Imagine a group of strangers. They don't know anything about each other, and the only thing that they all have in common is that they have realized that keeping their money in one centralized place, like a bank, is perhaps not the smartest idea. After all, banks can get hacked, as they have been many times before. In addition, this group of strangers are tired of the high banking fees added to their transactions and they want a new, improved system.

So, they decide to create it on their own. This is the birth of the blockchain.

They don't want to share their personal information with others so they use secret identities. For this example let's keep things simple, and use a group of 14 people all who use numbers from 1 to 14 as their secret identities.

The individuals in this group each own a computer, and this network of computers (which are also referred to as 'nodes') and the system as a whole is the blockchain. Their secret identities are their usernames or user IDs and the money on their balances is in cryptocurrencies. In order to create their own system, the one thing they will share is their account balance. Every participant types in a spreadsheet how much money each person has.

Now we have a group that only knows two things about the other people – how much money they have, and a list of secret identities. This is when the action begins, and transactions start happening.

It all starts with Person #14 wanting to buy a product from Person #6 for €25. Person #14 lets the network know, "I'm sending €25 to Person #6!"

Then, all of the computers check whether Person #14 has enough money to make this transaction.

Person #14 is on the right financial track and does have enough money. All of the computers in the group now confirm that Person #14 sent €25 to Person #6 in this transaction.

This also means that they must update the account balances – Person #14 now has €25 less and Person #6 has €25 more. Now that the transaction is settled, Person #6 gives Person #14 the product.

But what would have happened if Person #14 wasn't as wealthy and didn't have enough funds to send €25? Then once she attempted the transaction, all of the other computers would see that Person #14 didn't have enough money, and they would not allow this transaction to take place.

This process continues for sometime, where transactions are recorded within the blocks and are broadcast to the network, where they will get validated by the nodes. The filling up of the block with transactions illustrates the building of a blockchain, one block at a time.

Transactions, Hash Function and Hash Value

In the case of any cryptocurrency, for instance Bitcoin, the nodes (or computers) in the network will first validate that an account has the amount that is needed to send, and if that amount is available, the transaction will be included in a block, which will be attached to the previous block of transactions.

Everyone who uses cryptocurrency has a wallet, which keeps the owners' address, or public key. Every public key has a corresponding private key, which is for the owner of the wallet to keep safe (please refer to page 50). The wallet also keeps a record of all transactions and balances. Every transaction that is made is signed with a private key. Both a private key and the transaction details, including to whom the amount of cryptocurrency is to be sent, is kept on the cryptocurrency software installed on the phone or computer of the wallet owner. When the transaction is sent, along with it is sent a digital signature, which will be validated by the network of computers (or nodes).

Once the transaction has been validated, it gets included into a "block," along with many other transactions.

For every transaction, a hash or hash value (see page 50) is produced using the hash function, which is the 'Machine' that creates the hash value. The hash function is a complex mathematical equation that takes an amount of text or data and creates a character string of a certain length (for instance, 64 characters). The same exact character string will be produced every time that exact data set is sent through the hash function, but if even one number is changed, a completely different character string will be produced. This is how the blockchain can confirm if a transaction has, or has not, been tampered with.

INPUT

Transaction

Any length of data

⬇

OUTPUT #A

391efa0c34aea8f0f96d...

Unique hash value, always the same length

Understanding a Bitcoin transaction

1 Jimmy wants to send 2 bitcoin to Megan

He broadcasts his transaction request to the bitcoin blockchain
– a decentralized database run by a world-wide network of computers

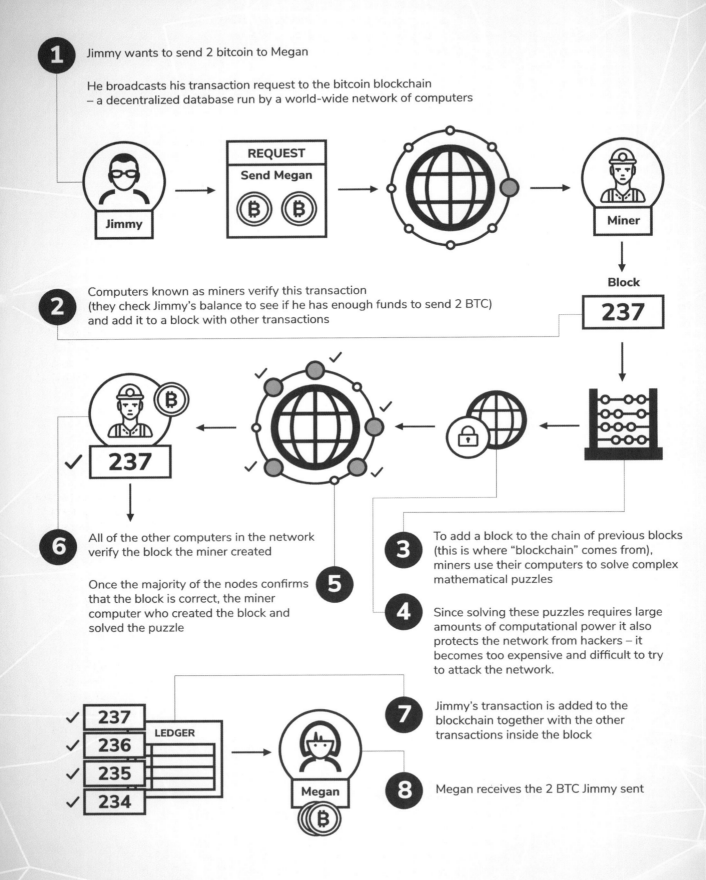

2 Computers known as miners verify this transaction
(they check Jimmy's balance to see if he has enough funds to send 2 BTC)
and add it to a block with other transactions

Block

237

6 All of the other computers in the network verify the block the miner created

Once the majority of the nodes confirms that the block is correct, the miner computer who created the block and solved the puzzle

5

3 To add a block to the chain of previous blocks (this is where "blockchain" comes from), miners use their computers to solve complex mathematical puzzles

4 Since solving these puzzles requires large amounts of computational power it also protects the network from hackers – it becomes too expensive and difficult to try to attack the network.

7 Jimmy's transaction is added to the blockchain together with the other transactions inside the block

8 Megan receives the 2 BTC Jimmy sent

237
236 **LEDGER**
235
234

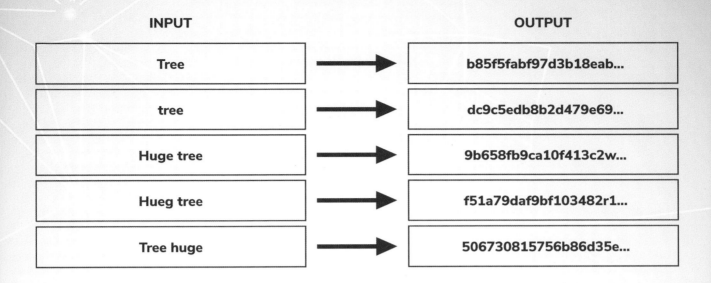

INPUT		OUTPUT
Tree	→	b85f5fabf97d3b18eab...
tree	→	dc9c5edb8b2d479e69...
Huge tree	→	9b658fb9ca10f413c2w...
Hueg tree	→	f51a79daf9bf103482r1...
Tree huge	→	506730815756b86d35e...

Every block includes, as part of its data, a hash of the previous block. That's what makes it part of the chain. So, if one small part of the previous block was tampered with, the current block's hash would have to change, and every block after that. This would be too difficult for someone to manipulate. The use of hash functions, and blockchain in general, guarantees that the system functions efficiently, that all of the blocks contain the right information, and that no one can secretly alter the transactions and write on them that they have millions of Euros instead of tens of Euros in their accounts.

Block Headers, Mining and Rewards

By now you know that 'blocks' are the units of the blockchain and is the unit in which data is structured. The computers that process the blocks are called miners. Adding transactions to the blockchain needs considerable computer processing power as miners compete to solve complex mathematical problems involving hash functions, and are rewarded for processing, validating and sealing the blocks of transactions.

> **Fun fact:** On the Bitcoin blockchain, one block contains more than 500 transactions and the average blocksize is about 1MB. Bitcoin Cash has a blocksize of 8MB allowing more transactions per second (tps)

A block is composed of a block header plus a list of transactions. The block header contains a summary of information about the block, including a hash of the transactions within the block, block version number, a timestamp, the hash used in the previous block, the Merkle Root (see explanation on page 65), and the difficulty. That is a lot of hashing! Also included within the block header is an arbitrary number called a nonce which is a random string of numbers chosen by the miner. When a working nonce is found, the block is solved and this is the 'Proof of Work'.

Mining is about allowing a blockchain to become a decentralized entity, and not solely about creating new cryptocurrency.

Merkle Tree

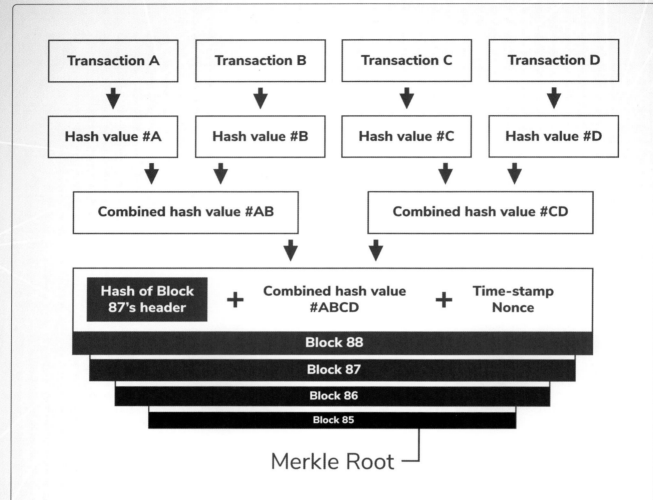

All of the transactions that make up a block are run through an algorithm that produces encrypted codes, also known as hash values, to these transactions. These hash values are combined with each other into a data structure called a Merkle Tree. The result of this combining and hashing is added to the block's header, together with a hash of the previous block's header and a time-stamp. To add the block to the blockchain, miners have to solve mathematical puzzles by finding a number called the nonce that would satisfy the requirements of the puzzle when added to the block's header and run through a hash function. Once a miner finds a nonce that satisfies the requirement, then the block is added to the blockchain, and the miner receives a reward.

Blockchain Blocks

Block Height 277316
Header Hash: 00000000000000078d8d63mr7f56fdn46d620ckshr97

Previous Block Hash:
0000000000000002hsgf6839d9g87f64md8vgfxm97cmhd9djds73jf7

Timestamp: 2013-12-27 23:11:54

Difficulty:1180923195.26

Nonce 924591725

Merkle Root:
823nf7732hi20732jhjd273351vzde630ld8d7a6d8f7ds6nc61b3v

HEADER

Transactions

Block Height 277315
Header Hash: 00000000000000087s78287r6ftf43o8q76dtr12889f892hh

Previous Block Hash:
0000000000000098uhr9u8gf7tf78e8gfgbog7643gp8c932yrc179g

Timestamp: 2013-12-27 22:57:18

Difficulty:1180923195.26

Nonce 4215469401

Merkle Root:
8x92yehd98w62fdlapiu265dqf7w729frj836hd87s8s73he73hd86gfs

HEADER

Transactions

Block Height 277315
Header Hash: 00000000000000087s78287r6ftf43o8q76dtr12889f892hh

Previous Block Hash:
000000000000000f1e3tfy32309uc7gef86wtfg4938y5rgh7fg7f3298

Timestamp: 2013-12-27 22:55:40

Difficulty:1180923195.26

Nonce 3797028665

Merkle Root:
9047uf9ehf9w7tr8643ge490gy97fg349f87r0gurgfew89fhsgcvwero

HEADER

Transactions

Mining in Bitcoin

As stated, miners validate new transactions and record them on the blockchain, a global ledger, and the solution found is called the Proof-Of-Work or PoW. This 'proof' proves that a miner spent a lot of time and resources to solve the problem. When a block is 'solved', the transactions contained are considered confirmed, and the Bitcoin attached to those transactions can be spent by the recipients of these transactions. Currently, it takes 10 minutes for a Bitcoin transaction to be confirmed.

A nonce is a random, arbitrary number that will be used just once to find a hash below the target number which is calculated based on the difficulty. Proof of Work, which is the consensus algorithm for Bitcoin mining, takes an input consisting of the Merkle Root, timestamp, previous block hash and a couple of other things, plus a nonce which is this completely random number. If the output results in a hash which is smaller than the target hash, the miner (computer or node) will win the block and the consensus will be reached.

The miner that is able to find the working nonce is awarded the block and paid in cryptocurrency (in this case Bitcoin) plus transaction fees. The amount of Bitcoins created decreases every 4 years, or every 210,000 blocks, to be precise. Today, a newly created block creates 12.5 Bitcoins. This number will keep going down until no more Bitcoins will be issued, around 2140, when around 21 million Bitcoins will have been created. After this date, no more Bitcoins will be issued.

Transactions

Transaction is made

Request to create the transaction is broadcast to the network of computers (nodes).

The nodes check the transaction and the user's balance, to confirm that everything is legitimate

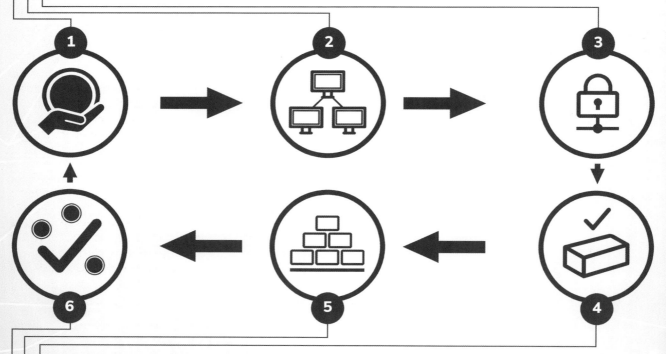

Confirmed transactions are added into blocks

After solving a mathematical puzzle, the block is added to the existing blockchain, recording and time-stamping the transactions inside the block permanently and transparently to the database

The transaction is completed and the money is sent

Problems With Mining

The Proof-of-Work (PoW) system was the first system used for reaching consensus within the blockchain, meaning it was used to make sure that all of the participants agreed upon one thing and to keep the system organized.

This system works well, as it makes it easy to validate whether a block is correct or not. It also presents a way to introduce new money into circulation, and makes cheating extremely difficult. It does everything it has to do, but there are some drawbacks.

One of the main problems is that since mining requires a lot of computing power, and thus a lot of energy, it is not very environment-friendly. For example, Bitcoin mining by itself has consumed more electricity than over 4,000,000 households in the US in 2017.

Another big problem with mining is that there are large mining pools that have formed over time, which control the majority of the mining and thus make the system less decentralized. For example, with Bitcoin, more than 80% of the mining power is in the hands of the top 8 mining pools (mining pools are platforms where miners can combine their hashing power to create one giant miner that can efficiently mine blocks, and receive payments regularly in proportion to their mining power, instead of waiting years to mine their one block individually.)

In the beginning, people could use their regular laptops for mining, but now there are enormous warehouses full of special computers that are meant especially for mining (they are called ASICs or Application-Specific Integrated Circuits). These computers are completely useless besides mining, in which they perform extremely well. These large mining farms have made it impossible for individual miners to mine profitably and so the only way to earn money is to join a mining pool.

Since PoW systems require difficult mathematical puzzles to be solved, which take a lot of time, then this system is not the fastest. In order to solve these issues, other consensus algorithms have been created by blockchains.

Blockchains and Algorithms

Before we go any further, what is an algorithm? Computers know what to do because they have written lines of instruction called code, and before you can write code, you need an algorithm. Basically, an algorithm is a list of rules to follow in order to solve a problem.

As already stated, before blocks can be added to the blockchain, they have to be validated. There are many different types of block validation, or in tech terms, 'consensus algorithms'. These algorithms are the cornerstones for every blockchain network and keep the network in harmony, not in chaos.

Blockchain has many characteristics including decentralization, stability, security, and non-modifiability, and the consensus algorithm plays a crucial role in maintaining the purpose, safety and efficiency of each blockchain. None of the consensus algorithms are exactly the same, though a few share similar concepts.

Here's a brief overview of the Top 10 most popular algorithms, and a sample of which blockchains use them:

1. Proof of Work - Bitcoin, Ethereum, and Monero

Bitcoin's founder created Proof of Work, where miners configure their computers to solve very intense puzzles in order to create the next block. When they solve that puzzle (with Bitcoin, once every 10 minutes), they are given a reward in either coins or tokens. Bitcoin has become so valuable, entire countries are setting up huge factories to create blocks and claim rewards. Places that have free power have a tremendous advantage, as the machines required to mine these blocks suck up unbelievable amounts of power. A decommissioned power plant in Australia was recently purchased solely for the purpose of Bitcoin mining.

Pros:

Anybody can make money from their idle computer. The amount depends on which coin, the type of computer, and cost to power it. There are special mining computers which are solely made for mining cryptocurrency. If you are trying to compete against miners using specialized mining hardware, it may not be profitable to even try.

Cons:

PoW is slow. Blocks occur every few minutes, or whatever the code defines. PoW is very un-ecofriendly. Many profitable coins are now dominated by large companies that have sprung up for the sole purpose of mining these coins (Bitcoin or Ethereum). If any one or two companies have more than 51% of the "hashrate" (think of it as blockchain speed), they essentially are now in control of the chain. They could infuse a new code with different rules, causing the chain to split, with many network nodes configured automatically to stay with the biggest chain (this is known as a fork).

2. Proof of Stake - NEO, DASH, and NavCoin

Instead of mining, people who hold the coins belonging to the network have the option of being "minters". A designated third party creates the blocks, which allows the minters run software on their computers that act as validators. It's much less energy intensive and requires no special hardware, just coins. The more coins you have "staked" in the blockchain, the higher the chance you have at being selected (at random) to validate a block.

Pros:

Any coin holder can be a validator, as long as you are willing to lock up your coins and not spend them. PoS is much more energy efficient, and much faster and there can be several blocks per minute. Proof of Stake is much safer, as to perform a 51% attack you would need to have 51% of all the coins, and attacking the network would only cause your own investment to be depleted.

Cons:

Your coins are locked up in a deposit when you are "minting", but you can pull them out at any time. There are some complex theoretical ways to still attack this type of network.

3. Delegated Proof of Stake - EOS, Bitshares, and Lisk

There is a major difference in this system as compared to the previous two listed. Instead of everybody having a chance at validating a block, only a small number of machines on the network are selected, by a vote. This way, it is much easier for a handful of computers to talk to one another to compare blocks and validation, in a much more efficient way. If one validator starts to fail, they are voted out of circulation and replaced by another computer on the network. Instead of miners competing with each other, in DPoS they all work together to solve the block puzzle, creating blocks much, much faster.

Pros:

DPoS is fast! Blocks take less than one second to be created. The entire network is working together instead of against each other. This type of network is much more easily expanded, since it is so much more inclusive.

Cons:

This system is partially centralized and controlled. In addition, it is fairly new and untested against attacks.

4. Proof of Authority - POA Network, Ethereum's Kovan Testnet

This consensus algorithm is pretty much the same as the client/server relationship. There is one authority in charge of everything, and the clients can just read the information (if allowed). This is best used in private corporate chains. Additional conditions to become an authority can be specified, including identity management and verification, in contrast to the previously mentioned algorithms, where the only identity on the network is often a wallet address or IP address/port.

Pros:

PoA is fast, reliable, and trusted.

Cons:

The community has no vote or control. The creator of the chain can implement updates at will or decide not to create any updates at all.

5. Proof of Burn - Binance Coin, Counterparty, and Slimcoin

The concept of Proof of Burn is the following: Instead of being rewarded for solving puzzles, the miners are meant to send coins to an irretrievable address, to be lost forever. The concept is by decreasing the supply of coins, the value of the remaining ones increase. More often than not, the practice of "burning" coins is something done by the developers rather than the community. Blockchain ICOs often burn any unsold tokens remaining. Binance burns some of its profits every quarter, to ensure its coin gains value.

Pros:

With Proof of Burn, scarcity drives the value of the remaining coins up.

Cons:

Once coins are burned, they are lost forever which helps the ecosystem, but there is no direct reward to miners for burning coins.

6. Directed Acyclic Graph - IOTA, Hashgraph, and Nano

Participants in this network that want to send a transaction, are first required to do a small proof of work, in which they verify two previous transactions that occurred before. In theory, this tangle can accelerate to near-instant speeds. Unlike traditional servers, the more users that are logged on, the faster the transaction speeds get. Each of the blockchain networks that use DAG has their own unique take on how to organize transactions, so read into each project more for further information.

Pros:

Extremely fast, once it gets going.

Cons:

With little activity, transactions will not get processed. Instead of 51%, only 33% of active traffic is required to take over this kind of network.

7. Byzantine Fault Tolerance - Ripple, Stellar, and Dispatch

With Byzantine Fault Tolerance, pre-selected validators are in charge of the network and no miners or community contributors are required. With that said, Stellar allows anyone to become a validator, while Ripple itself decides who validates blocks on their network. These are centralized services using blockchain technology.

Pros:

These are very fast, private networks

Cons:

Validators are merely using these blockchain networks, they are not part of them.

8. Proof of Space/Capacity - Burst

Although, only one coin currently uses this, it is an interesting algorithm. It allows people to mine using spare hard drive space, instead of CPU/GPU cycles. Your hard drive space is filled up with small amounts of random files that act like lottery tickets. The network elects a winner every defined number of seconds (or minutes) and gives them a coin reward. It takes tiny fractions of energy (5 watts) to power a hard drive, compared to 100+ watts of a single GPU or 1200+ watts of an ASIC (specialized mining hardware developed just for Bitcoin and other major coins).

9. Proof of Activity - Decred

This is a combination of both PoW and PoS. Currently only Decred uses it and the pros and cons remain to be seen.

10. Proof of Elapsed Time - Hyperledger Sawtooth

Every participant in the network is assigned a random time in each block, and whoever's time runs out first, gets to create the next block. This network is called permissioned because prospective participants must identify themselves to the network who will decide whether or not to let them participate. As clients on this network must be identified, and their code must have passed verification trust, to avoid simply exploiting the time on your network node to trigger sooner. The pros and cons

There are still other algorithm, which include:

- Proof of Importance
- Proof of Reputation
- Proof of Weight
- Proof of Evolution
- Tendermint
- CASPER
- Distributed Byzantine Fault Tolerance
- SPECTRE
- and so many more...

Rapid Fire Q&A

What is a blockchain?

The blockchain is a number of computers around the world who are all linked (networked) with each other and record information all at the same time. This information is recorded in 'blocks' and every time more blocks are added, it makes a chain. The blockchain is also digital ledger in which transactions are recorded chronologically (by time and date) and publicly (everyone can see it).

How does it work?

There is a network, or group, of computers which all work together to store and validate information – in other words, make sure the information is correct and true. When new data is given to the network, it is validated (or said to be correct and true), and stored in blocks, and these blocks are also validated and added to the existing chain of blocks.

What are the benefits?

Blockchain technology's benefits include faster transaction speeds, lower fees, increased security, transparency, and automation.

How did it start?

The first time something resembling a blockchain was described was in the 1970s. The first public blockchain was created with the invention of Bitcoin in 2009 by an anonymous person or group named Satoshi Nakamoto.

What can it be used for?

Blockchain can be used for transferring money and data, keeping records, creating contracts, automating businesses, authentication, proving ownership, voting and much more.

Can I get my account or wallet hacked?

If you do everything like you should – use a strong password, act smart, and not share your personal information then you will not lose your money or information.

What are cryptocurrencies?

Cryptocurrencies are the most popular function of blockchain technology. They are the cash of the internet.

What is decentralization?

Decentralization means that instead of one central computer or server that records payments or transactions and processes data, there are many different places where a copy of the information and transactions are stored. Most companies use centralized systems which are easier to break into allowing unauthorized parties to modify or steal information that they should not have access to in the first place.

Why is blockchain good?

Blockchain offers better security and safety through decentralization and cryptography. It also offers high-speed transactions with low costs, and no third parties are required for transactions.

What is cryptography?

Cryptography is a way to hide and send information using secret codes and strings of characters.

What are encryption and decryption?

Encryption is a cryptographic practice of using keys to scramble information to resemble nonsense. Decryption is the practice of converting this nonsense back into the original information.

What is hashing?

Hashing is a cryptographic function that takes information and gives an output which is unique. These outputs are called hashes, and cannot be altered, or replicated, and they are irreversible, unlike encryptions.

What are keys?

Keys are long numbers that are used for encrypting and decrypting data, and a type of code. The strength of the encryption, or code, is determined by the length of the key used.

What are wallets?

Wallets are used for storing cryptocurrency and the public and private keys to your account. They store the proof that you are the owner of cryptocurrencies, or digital money.

What are public and private keys?

Public and private keys are used in asymmetrical cryptography. Data which is encrypted with a public key can only be decrypted with the corresponding private key and vice-versa.

What is the difference between coins and tokens?

Coins are cryptocurrencies that have their own blockchain and are meant for only transferring money (for instance, Bitcoin has its own blockchain). Tokens are built on an already existing blockchain and are meant to have other uses besides transferring money, like having access to video games made by the company creating the tokens.

What is FIAT?

FIAT is money, or currency, which is issued by the governments of countries. For instance, the currency of the United States is called the US Dollar (USD), the European Union currency is the Euro (EUR), and the currency of the United Kingdom is the Great British Pound (GBP).

What are smart contracts?

Smart contracts are automated contracts that work on the blockchain. They are "If-This-Then-That" functions, so if you have a contract with your mom that you will get one Bitcoin if you do your homework online, once the computer knows you have done your online homework, it will tell the contract that you have done your part of the agreement, and you will be paid by your mother who will receive a confirmation that the homework is finished. Cool, huh?

What are nodes?

Nodes are the computers that take part in the blockchain network. They store and validate the data presented to the blockchain.

A full node is a complete copy of the entire blockchain and is able to verify all transactions and blocks since the beginning.

What are miners?

Miners are computers that compete to add blocks to the blockchain. They do the work. In return for their work, they'll receive rewards in the means of cryptocurrencies. Anyone can mine using special computers, called miners.

A miner creates blocks in the blockchain, which the nodes keep forever. The miner works on transactions by coming up with the best way to store that information. This information is the unique output or hashes. Miners spend minutes working on a problem, but nodes keep that result for forever and verify it with others.

Miners don't need to know about any other blocks except for the last one it worked on, but nodes need to know all of the blocks. All miners are nodes, but not all nodes are miners.

What are ITOs/ICOs?

ITOs/ICOs are Initial Token/Coin Offerings. They are normally used by start-ups that wish to integrate blockchain technology into their business and are looking to raise funding for their ventures. They are essentially IPOs (Initial Public Offerings) on the blockchain.

What is a block?

A block is a collection of transactions. Blocks are stored on the blockchain in a chronological order to create a chain of blocks – the blockchain.

What is Proof-of-Work?

Proof-of-Work is the system used in most cryptocurrency protocols. Computers use their computing power to solve mathematical puzzles in order to validate data, also called mining.

Why is blockchain all of a sudden so popular?

Blockchain technology gained popularity mostly thanks to the invention of Bitcoin. A lot of people saw potential in it as a very useful currency and others saw how this coin rose from nothing to thousands in the span of few years.

CONCLUSION

What You Learned

In this book we covered the basics of blockchain and cryptocurrencies:

> What blockchain means, how was it created, why it matters, what it consists of, what makes it unique and useful, and why you should care.

> We explained cryptocurrencies, how they work, and why are they so volatile

> We explored smart contracts, how they function, what are the advantages, and what they can be used for.

> We went over cryptography to better understand how safety is ensured on the blockchain.

> We briefly talked about the topic of ITOs/ICOs and what are they.

> And, we did a rapid-fire Q&A to provide you with fast answers for frequently asked questions.

Now you have a good grounding on cryptocurrency and blockchain, the next time there is a conversation about these topics, you can actively participate in them. You should fully understand what cryptocurrencies and smart contracts are, the meaning of the words "miner" and "FIAT", and you should not be dragged into ITOs or ICOs that are scams. You may not be a blockchain expert, yet, but you do know more than the average person.

If you wish to get more information or give us feedback visit:
https://www.saviidigital.com/cryptoforbeginners
or e-mail us: **education@saviidigital.com**

If you bought this book from Amazon, you can leave your feedback to the Amazon review section.

Thank You for reading,
Savii Digital

SAVII PUBLISHING
CRYPTO AND BLOCKCHAIN BOOKS

CRYPTOCURRENCY AND BLOCKCHAIN ACTIVITY BOOK

Activity buffs of all ages can learn while drawing, coloring, solving puzzles and immersing in adventures with our Cryptocurrency and Blockchain Activity Book.

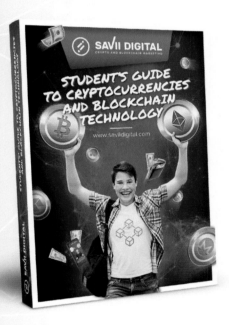

STUDENT'S GUIDE TO CRYPTOCURRENCIES AND BLOCKCHAIN TECHNOLOGY

For older kids, we recommend the Student's Guide to Cryptocurrencies and Blockchain Technology. This book is full of illustrative pictures and infographics that give the curious teenager a brief overview of crypto vocabulary and the terms related to this space.

MEET BOB THE BLOCKTRAIN

Meet Bob the Blocktrain is a playful invitation to the happy world of crazy cryptocurrencies and boundless blockchain fun. Bob the Blocktrain, with the help of happy-go-lucky nodes and miners will transport the eager listener or beginner story reader through the learning process.

See more from Savii Publishing:
www.saviidigital.com/books

44097047R00047

Printed in Poland
by Amazon Fulfillment
Poland Sp. z o.o., Wrocław